Reflections

Transgender at 7,
Out at 84

EVE BURCHERT

REFLECTIONS: TRANSGENDER AT 7, OUT AT 84

Copyright © 2018 Atlantic Publishing Group, Inc.

1405 SW 6th Avenue • Ocala, Florida 34471 • Phone 800-814-1132 • Fax 352-622-1875
Website: www.atlantic-pub.com • Email: sales@atlantic-pub.com
SAN Number: 268-1250

Library of Congress Cataloging-in-Publication Number: 2018023355

E-book ISBN: 9781620235249

Printed in the United States of America

PROJECT MANAGER AND EDITOR: Danielle Lieneman
INTERIOR LAYOUT AND JACKET DESIGN: Nicole Sturk

Reduce. Reuse.
RECYCLE.

Over the years, we have adopted a number of dogs from rescues and shelters. First there was Bear and after he passed, Ginger and Scout. Now, we have Kira, another rescue. They have brought immense joy and love not just into our lives, but into the lives of all who met them.

We want you to know a portion of the profits of this book will be donated in Bear, Ginger and Scout's memory to local animal shelters, parks, conservation organizations, and other individuals and nonprofit organizations in need of assistance.

– Douglas & Sherri Brown,
President & Vice-President of Atlantic Publishing

What are little girls made of?
Sugar and spice and everything nice
That's what little girls are made of
What are little boys made of?
Slugs and snails and puppy dogs' tails
That's what little boys are made of.

—English nursery rhyme

Table of Contents

Introduction

The normal male (normal by his genetic inheritance) has his masculine build and voice, an ample supply of androgen, satisfactory potency, a sperm count that assures fertility, feels himself to be a man, is sexually attracted to women, and would be horrified to wear female clothes or "change his sex." He is often husband and father, works in a job or profession in accord with his sex and gender that is never questioned legally or socially.

The genetically normal female presents the opposite picture. She feels, looks, acts, and functions as a woman, wants to be nothing else, usually marries and has children. She dresses and makes up to be attractive to men, and her sex and gender are never doubted either by society or by the law.

Such more or less perfect symphony of the sexes is the rule. Yet, disturbances may occur more often than is usually assumed. Unfortunately, our conventions and our laws have no understanding, no tolerance for those in whom nature or life (nature or nurture) have created a dissonance in their sexuality ...

The transsexual (TS) male or female is deeply unhappy as a member of the sex (or gender) to which he or she was assigned by the anatomical structure of the body, particularly the genitals.

— Dr. Harry Benjamin, *The Transsexual Phenomenon*, 1966[1]

There is little that society takes for granted more than the separation of people into two sex categories, "male" and "female." Yet, when we try to define differences based on sex, problems and inconsistencies immediately arise.

At birth, a cursory examination is made of a baby's genitals. If the doctor sees a small penis, the parents are told: "It's a boy!" That was what my parents were told when I was born.

If the doctor sees a small vagina, the baby is declared a girl. From this initial declaration, most people are sent off on two different tracks in life through the process of development. We can think about gender as the set of different behaviors that society expects of persons labeled either male or female. For example, girls wear pink and dresses; boys are in blue and trousers. Boys are expected to play with trucks; girls might play with dolls. The differences go on and on, dictating the classes that students are encouraged to take in school and the careers they might pursue after. Is the significance of being born with a penis or a vagina so great that a person's future destiny should be dictated accordingly?

My parents were told I was a boy in 1933. Since then, conceptions of sex have become less fixed. Rather than an immutable trait, gender is becoming choosable in culture. Manhood and womanhood are lifestyle choices open to anyone, regardless of the genitals with which they are born. We now know that social customs and practices — not biology — are what make birth order, birth parents, skin tone, or genitals relevant to one's ability to perform a job or adopt a lifestyle. Liberated from legal constraints and archaic stereotypes, our social identity can flow from our soul and

---

1. Benjamin, 1966

our experience, not from our anatomy or birth status. Equal opportunity means that, from birth onward, people are people first; free to choose the culture and social applications that they like.

Martine Rothblatt, America's highest-paid female CEO who came out as transgender at age 40, expressed perfectly my own thoughts on transgenderism in her book, *The Apartheid of Sex*. According to Rothblatt, the guiding principle of transgenderism is that people should be free to change, either temporarily or permanently, the sex type to which they were assigned since infancy. Transgenderism favors the continuum nature of sex types because even if a sex type was real at birth, it can change at will during one's life.[2]

A variety of terms are used to describe individuals who challenge norms through their own gender presentation. During most of this book, I rely on the word "transgender." The word transsexual is used at times to refer to individuals who use hormones and sometimes plastic surgery to change their anatomy with a goal of presenting the sex opposite of the one they were assigned at birth. This term has recently fallen out of favor, as it's considered impolite to ask whether someone has had surgery on their genitals. There are also cross-dressers who use attitude, clothing, and perhaps makeup to give the appearance of belonging to the opposite sex, or to an androgynous middle ground. Cross-dressers may enjoy presenting as a different gender, but not yearn to be that in everyday life.

While one's gender may be an individual choice, Rothblatt also addresses the purpose of a growing transgender movement. She, like Benjamin at the beginning of this chapter, finds that transgender people of all types normally report a great need to express a gender identity different from the one society assigned them at their moment of birth.

Today, we go about the matter of sex backwards. A male or female label is first imposed upon us without choice. We are then trained to adopt a set of appropriate gender behaviors, whether we like them or not. However, feminism, technology, and transgenderism have debunked the myth of a

---

2. Rothblatt, 1995

world divided by the dichotomy of male and female. Life has much more gender potential than we imagine.

I initially learned about the potential of altering one's physical nature when I read about the first publicized sex change surgery, which occurred in Denmark in 1952. The operation was conducted on George Jorgensen, a young American who later became Christine Jorgensen. My discovery of this event awoke in me all the feelings and wants I had experienced since early in my childhood.

For most of my life, I have lived as a man. I went to school as a man, joined the military as a man, and launched a career as a man. I got married as a man and started a family. Then, in April of 2017, at the age of 84, I began living as a transgender woman; there was a lot more to my soul than the masculine person society had forced me to become. There was a woman who needed to be expressed.

The story that follows relates the journey of Eberhard. It is a story that begins in Marienburg, Germany at the height of World War II and concludes in Florida in the 21st century. It is a story that includes meeting Adolf Hitler, bombings, a stint in professional soccer, immigration to America, a career in the steel industry, marriage to two different women for a total of 61 years, and a transgender existence since the age of 7. It is my life story.

Chapter 1
A Prussian Childhood

I was born on February 19, 1933 in Koenigsberg, East Prussia, Germany. Koenigsberg was the easternmost large city in Germany, with a population of over 300,000 and a seaport located southwest of Lithuania at the Baltic Sea. It was the capital city of the German state of East Prussia. Teutonic knights, who came to Prussia to spread Christianity, originally founded the city in the 13th century. At the time of my birth, my father stationed there as a member of the German army.

On December 21, 1937, my sister Marianne came into the world. I was 4 years old at the time; my older brother, Detlef, was 6. When my new little sister came home from the hospital, adorably dressed in her little pink baby outfit, my mother asked both of us boys to kiss her. I refused. Although my thoughts about my gender were not fully developed, I think I protested out of envy; she was the girl I wanted to be.

My feelings solidified around age 7, and ever since then, I dreamt of being a girl. I envied those who were allowed to express femininity, both then and throughout my long life. However, when I was young, my desire to be a girl only simmered in my thoughts. Transgenderism was virtually unheard of, and many much more important events competed for my attention.

On September 1, 1939, Germany invaded Poland, marking the beginning of World War II. I was only 6 years old, but wartime meant that everyone became involved. I helped at my mother's family farm, I was required to join the Hitler Youth, and I eventually became a bicycle messenger for the Nazi party. Throughout all of this, I also grew up like any child. I recall that I was very jealous of the Hitler Youth girls, known as *Bund Deutscher Mädel*, or League of German Girls. Still, I had no way to express this. My wartime experiences were followed by my family's flight from the marauding Russian troops in early 1945, which created a climate that was anything but conducive to feminine apparel or makeup.

My birthplace is no longer part of Germany, but is nowadays the Russian city of Kaliningrad. At the Yalta Conference following World War II, the entire state of East Prussia was separated from Germany, with the northern part given to Russia and the southern part given to Poland. Twelve million ethnic Germans were ordered to leave their homeland and relocate to Germany. But my family left Koenisgberg before then. We moved to Marienburg, West Prussia, in 1942. The city has since been renamed Malbork and is now part of Poland. For my family, Marienburg was where we would experience the collapse of Germany from the onslaught of the Russian troops at the end of World War II.

Of course, when we moved to Marienburg, we knew nothing of this dangerous future. Our first few years in the city were exciting. In 1943, when I turned 10 years old, I was required — as all children were — to join the Hitler Youth. I had been looking forward to that moment with great excitement, as it was a rite of passage in wartime Germany. I loved my new uniform, which consisted of black shorts, a brown shirt with epaulets, a white belt, a shoulder strap on my right side, and a scarf with little knot around my neck. The squadron to which I was assigned sang inspiring political songs and went camping in the forest. We also made ourselves useful, collecting splinters of bombs following the frequent air attacks. We were told that the scrap metal could be melted to create raw material for tanks, airplanes, and other weapons.

After several months of the so-called basic training, I volunteered to transfer to a drum and bugle corps. Here, I was issued a large kettledrum, with a diameter of approximately 30 inches, and four drumsticks. As the drummer, I was at the forefront of our parades, which was quite fun. On other occasions, we would march from neighborhood to neighborhood, making lots of noise and using a bullhorn to alert the public of the dangers of bomb attacks.

It turned out that I was in for a very special event. During the early part of the war, every child in Hitler Youth went through a formal inauguration process. The ceremonies always took place somewhere grand that symbolized Hitler's political ambitions. When I was initiated, the chosen location was Marienburg Castle. The castle is one of the world's largest, complete with a moat, drawbridges, and a regal courtyard surrounded by cobblestones. Torches held by an SS honor guard illuminated the arched halls. We rehearsed for many hours before the moment of a lifetime finally arrived.

On the day of our inauguration, there was a big parade, and Adolf Hitler himself came to inspect the thousands of assembled youth. This was where my special moment of honor came in. A girl named Helga, from the *Bund Deutscher Mädel*, and I were chosen to present the Fuehrer with a bouquet of flowers. During his review of the assembled masses, he passed us in the reviewing stand. Movie cameras were directed at us as we each presented our salute to our country's chancellor. I recall vividly how he touched each of us on our shoulder and said, "You are our future." With that, we executed another "Heil Hitler" salute and stood at attention.

At the time, it was a joyous moment. That day, April 20, 1943, happened to be Hitler's birthday. Germany was enjoying the early success of the war, and its citizens were experiencing a pride not seen in decades. The country had not begun to feel the fear and insecurity that would come with the military's decline the next winter.

In hindsight, the fact that I met Hitler is shocking, to say the least. When I would move to the United States many years later, two of my first friends would be a Jewish couple who had survived Auschwitz. The horrors of the war cannot be understated, but as a child growing up in East Prussia, I had no understanding of such things.

In the spring of 1944, the year before Germany's defeat, my Hitler Youth career took another turn. I volunteered to become a messenger and was tasked with delivering memos from the headquarters to the front lines. For this purpose, I was issued a bicycle and routinely rode 50 kilometers each day. The course of the war had begun to change and the Soviet Russian army was beginning to advance west into Europe. To prevent this from happening, the *Volkssturm*, or German People's Army, was digging tank traps, known as *Panzergraben*, to keep Russian tanks from progressing west. Politicians believed that such traps would stop the Russian tanks and prevent an invasion of Germany.

My family's time in Marienburg wasn't completely dominated by the war. Every year and during summer vacations, my mother, Detlef, Marianne, and I would board a train toward Mehlsack, a small town in East Prussia where my maternal grandmother lived. The journey was about 200 kilometers.

My Uncle Paul would pick us up at the train station in Mehlsack in his two-horse carriage. From there, it was about an hour of travel to our family's country estate in Sonnwalde, which was a little outside of Mehlsack. In German tradition, the oldest heir inherits a parental estate while the remaining siblings must find other professions. My mother was one of seven children. Her sister was my aunt, Tante Josi, who had married Uncle Paul, who then became the owner of the estate. Their farm was one of the largest in their small village, and Uncle Paul became the *Ortsbauernleiter*, the village farm leader.

Their estate consisted of a handsome two-story home and two barns. The first barn, closer to the home, housed about 18 cows and six horses on the right side. On the left, there was an expansive pig stall and an area to store the nicer wagons and carriages. The primary barn was at the end of the farm. It had two drive-through entrances and exits, and was the storage place for the wheat, rye, barley, and hay. Behind this barn, there was a muddy pond, no more than three feet deep. To entertain ourselves, my brother and I would try to navigate across the pond using a pig's trough, although we never had much success; rather, our boating attempts usually resulted in us needing thorough baths. Beyond the storage barn, a wagon trail led about 500 meters to a junction. At the junction, there was a small brick house that was the home for the family who worked for my uncle on the farm. The trail continued, passing by several pastures that were neatly fenced with barbed wire. About three miles from the farm were the fields where the potatoes, wheat, and other grains grew. Even at my young age of 10, I was entrusted with a team of horses to haul manure out to the fields to improve the soil, or if it was harvest time, to pull the elongated ladder wagons that brought grain bundles from the fields to the farm.

For the time period, Uncle Paul had one of the most modern combines to mow and bundle rye, wheat, and barley. He would sit on the combine and control it while I led the four-horse team from the saddle of the left back horse. I was also entrusted to bring lunch out to the fields in an enameled coffee can, along with baskets full of sandwiches for the workers who would take a break to eat. I could usually perform all of these tasks without trouble, although once the rear axle of my liquid manure wagon caught the corner of the servants' house and tore out a couple of bricks.

After the harvests, Uncle Paul took his turn to use the community threshing machine alongside his barn. Everyone pitched in, carrying the grain bundles to the top of the thresher and then taking the 100-pound sacks of extracted grain back into the barn for storage. Once all of this was completed, we put Lottie and Hansi, Uncle Paul's favorite horses, to the flatbed wagon and drove seven kilometers to the town of Mehlsack, loaded down with the grain sacks. Upon arrival, we delivered them to a flourmill for further processing and sale. Sometimes, we would have to stop the wagon in order to hold onto Lottie when an automobile approached. She was not accustomed to cars and bolted when one came her way.

Early in January 1945, mother dressed my siblings and me in our Sunday best for our typical vacation trip to Sonnwalde. All of this sounded very pleasant and normal, except that Russian troops were rapidly advancing west and were reported to be just 50 kilometers from Mehlsack. Our family estate in Sonnwalde was northeast of Marienburg, making it even closer to the front lines. When we arrived at the train station in Mehlsack, we found that the trains westward were stormed by thousands of people, while our eastward trip had been comparatively lonesome.

We arrived at my grandmother's house just in time to observe a town in uproar as farmers were loading their horse-drawn wagons to flee west.

"What are you doing here? Get back to Marienburg!" everyone kept shouting at us.

It certainly was not a brilliant idea to undertake a vacation under these conditions. The Russian front was at the outskirts of Mehlsack when we arrived. In other words, we had traveled by train from an area that was set back from the front lines to a location from which evacuation would soon be impossible. We were lucky to catch the last train back to Marienburg.

Despite this brief escape, it would be only a matter of time before the war caught up with us.

Chapter 2
Escaping the War

There is no reason for concern," said Gauleiter Erich Koch, the governor of East Prussia. He had reassured us repeatedly that the German military would stem the flood of the invading Russian army. Although the German army had experienced a number of setbacks in 1944, we were told that the tide would turn.

Because of this overconfidence, Gauleiter Koch refused to authorize any preparation for the evacuation of East Prussia, even in the event of a hypothetical catastrophe. We were told that any German leaving East Prussia would be prosecuted by the state. This policy stemmed from the highly patriotic attitude that was common during wartime. Anyone who thought of evacuating could not be German, as no true German would dare to entertain the thought that East Prussia could fall into Russian Bolshevik hands. Not a meter of land would be relinquished without a price.

Such a nationalistic edict would prove tragic when the Russian invasion of Germany ultimately came about. By delaying the opportunity to evacuate East Prussia early and in an orderly manner, the government undoubtedly cost the lives of thousands.

Germany's apparent denial of the fact that it was losing the war affected every policy decision. If the country had wanted to stop Russian advances, it should have done everything in its power to build a back defensive line. However, Hitler viewed such a defensive measure as defeatism and continued to maintain his own directives. In December 1944, he even decided to withdraw divisions from the already thinly defended Eastern front in order to start the Ardennes offensive — also known as the Battle of the Bulge, an offensive attack on the western front in Belgium that was considered speculative by all experts and foolish under such conditions.

Rather than receiving the help and evacuation that we needed, the German population was inundated with illusions, each time justified with the argument: "It could not possibly happen that everything was for nothing." By this point, Germany had been at war for five years; no one wanted to believe that we would lose. Unfortunately, this argument was used to justify the prohibition of any evacuation of the civilian population; neither children nor luggage were to be shipped westward.

One of the German soldiers still fighting during this time was my father. The 14th and youngest child of his parents, he wasn't in line to inherit the large farm and flourmill. Instead, he enlisted into the German army, not long after World War I. He advanced through the ranks, ultimately achieving the rank of major. During World War II, he primarily fought against the Russians on the Eastern front and was wounded 13 times.

In the fall of 1944, a few months before the chaos reached Marienburg, there was a lull in the fighting, and my father sent a message to my mother, asking that she send me to the trenches. At the time, my father still had confidence in his unit and in Germany's military chances. Given this, I think he wanted to show me off to his unit.

I went as close as I could by train to his position in Russia. From there, he sent a motorcycle to pick me up and take me the final distance to his bunker and trenches. However, while the motorcycle driver was deployed to give me a ride, the Russians launched a counteroffensive and some of my father's territory was pushed a few miles back. After picking me up, the driver and I found ourselves on the motorcycle, dangerously close to enemy lines and drawing fire from the Russians. We made it to my father's trenches without harm, and I asked him to equip me with a rifle. Of course, he declined and tried to persuade me to go back to the supply units and the horses. I was 11 years old at the time.

My father's soldiers dedicated the following commemoration, translated from the German, to him for Christmas in 1944. It describes my visit to the front lines of the German fortifications ("Burchert Junior" refers to me).

REMEMBRANCES OF JUBARKAS (RUSSIA)

It was October in this year, as Iwan had penetrated the line, when we received orders at night to rush forward to aid in defense.

To cover the left flank, the brave soldiers dug their potholes along the banks of the Memel River, with a view toward north, where the enemy hordes in Jubarkas were ready to cross the river. It was just high time!

Despite organ, artillery, and tank firepower, and superior force, which was enormous, each attack was fought off during these wild days.

In the forest at his command post, the commander achieved the battles victory with safe improvised hand and skill. Nothing could interrupt his objective and our victory was assured.

However, when during the height of the attack, the general called by telephone, despite roars of detonating bombs, asked this and that, while we were crouched in our potholes, hardly a word could be understood, it was the masters wish deep down, leave me alone, for heavens' sake.

Suddenly, reinforcement arrived to support our weak positions. A motorcycle arrived hurriedly and brought Burchert Junior.

Come on, Dad, give me a rifle, shooting will be easy for me, I am determined to hold my own; come on, Dad, you will see. United persuasion succeeded to convince the boy that this was not the right place for him, and Dad smiled proudly.

The battle was over; the victory was ours thanks to the bravery and leadership skills. The F.E.B., when called upon, faithfully fulfilled its duty and proudly carries its name as "Fire Department" of the Division.

To our honored commander Major Burchert, at the occasion of the 6th wartime Christmas, submitted by [the names and ranks of all the men in my father's unit].

After I experienced much more war action than my father would have liked, I was escorted away from the front lines by motorcycle. I returned to Marienburg by train not long after, rejoining my mother and siblings.

Although I had received a sneak preview of Germany's ultimate collapse when I visited my father, life for the rest of our family back in our apartment on Hindenburg Strasse in Marienburg progressed rather normally. We received a Feldpost Karte (field postcard) from my father, who seemed full of optimism and reassurance. He wrote: "While we have endured a lot, we are confident of victory and are waiting for the secret weapon which will help us beat our enemy."

Unfortunately, my father's confidence was misguided. In 1944, the German front lines experienced a number of setbacks. On the Western Front, the English and American invasion forces, with their enormous superiority, had accomplished the landing in the Normandy. They had been able to penetrate the German western army, which was without air support, having only poor supplies and a confused leadership team. The Allies had overrun France and Belgium and progressed up to the German border. In Italy, the Allies had toppled the fascist government in 1943, and were advancing their fight northward, piece-by-piece, fighting German soldiers every step.

The conflict between the Germans and Russians in Eastern Europe, named Operation Barbarossa, can only be described as total war. When the Germans invaded the Soviet Union, they had initially made major territorial gains and captured millions of Soviet soldiers, many of whom were killed. However, the Soviets staged a major counteroffensive after the Battle of Moscow and were ready to afflict every ounce of pain and suffering back on the Germans.

Ilya Ehrenburg, a notable Soviet writer, distributed a number of pamphlets and fliers that described the way the Russians would come to treat the Germans:

> The Germans are not human beings. From now on the word German means to use the most terrible oath. From now on the word German strikes us to the quick. We shall not speak any more. We shall not get excited. We shall kill. If you have not killed at least one German a day, you have wasted that day ... If you cannot kill your German with a bullet, kill him with your bayonet. If there is calm on your part of the front, or if you are waiting for the fighting, kill a German in the meantime. If you leave a German alive, the German will hang a Russian and rape a Russian woman. If you kill one German, kill another — there is nothing more amusing for us than a heap of German corpses. Do not count days, do not count kilometers. Count only the number of Germans killed by you. Kill the German — that is your grandmother's request. Kill the German — that is your child's prayer. Kill the German — that is your motherland's loud request. Do not miss. Do not let through. Kill.[3]

In Marienburg and across other German towns that would soon be hit with war, three waves were converging: the retreat of a beaten German army, the unplanned flight of the civilian population, and the penetration of an enemy determined to use the ultimate cruelty. It could only be described as a recipe for disaster.

---

3. Weber, 1988-9

In the middle of January 1945, the Russian offensive broke loose against the front. In hindsight, it was hardly a surprise: the German defenses were as breakable as thin ice in spring. The country's once-strong military had weakened over the course of the war; German divisions now consisted of only a few hundred men. The tank units had been forced to destroy a third of their vehicles in order to conserve gasoline for those remaining. There was no one in a leadership position who had the courage to sweep Hitler's dilettante strategies off the table and assume leadership in order to hinder his senseless slaughter.

In Marienburg, January 23 began just like any other cold, snowy winter mornings we were accustomed to. A day previously, Grandma, who was now 80 years old, had arrived from Mehlsack to seek shelter. Our family gathered around the radio to listen to the special broadcast:

"Achtung, Achtung. Das Oberkommando der Wehrmacht gibt bekannt."

"Attention, Attention. The Superior Command of the Military announces the heroic Army under the command of General Guderian has stopped the enemy. There is no cause of concern."

If there was nothing to be concerned about, then why were the streets out of town suddenly jam-packed with refugees and military personnel? Something didn't seem right, but we didn't have much time to think — the next instant our building was rocked by artillery shells. The gable to the east collapsed under several hits. Amidst the chaos, Mother gave us a set of commands: "Quickly, kids: each pack a knapsack with your most important possessions; some underwear, socks and another shirt; we have to leave." It was 2 o'clock in the morning.

In a time of great anxiety, I managed to secretly pack my most treasured items, a blouse and a skirt I had been keeping in a special hiding place. Those items had been my dearest possessions for the previous few years. I had stolen them from my mother and rejoiced having something female that I could call my own. My mother did not know I had them nor did she ask me what I had packed in the early morning hours. That conflict would come later.

After we had all quickly packed our things, we ate a bite of food, not knowing when our next meal would come. Then we rose, leaving the food and cutlery at the table, and walked out the front door, not bothering to look back. The streets looked miserable, completely covered in ice, and the temperature hovered around 20 below zero on the Celsius scale — around minus 4 degrees Fahrenheit.

Our street, Hindenburg Strasse, was one of the main thoroughfares leading out of Marienburg towards the west. It was jammed with traffic of all sorts: horse-drawn wagons, military trucks, tanks, and people pulling sleds or pushing baby carriages through the snow. We also encountered the chaotic conditions of survival under the worst possible conditions. I will never forget passing a woman who was sitting in the snow, leaning against a tree with a dead baby in her arms. My mother tried to persuade her to come with us. The woman apathetically rejected, telling us that she wanted to die right there with her child.

Because Gauleiter Koch's had refused to permit any preparation for the evacuation of East Prussia, the population only started to take flight when the Russians penetrated the front and moved into our cities and towns. Now the streets and roads were crowded with fleeing divisions of convoys alongside escaping civilians.

As our trek westward continued, we met many small tradesmen and store owners who had set out on foot with small wagons, carrying their grand-mothers or their belongings. Very slowly, the East Prussian landscape passed by, like the scenery of a surrealistic film. There were more and more people trudging through the snow, and some appeared to have a difficult time separating themselves from their houses. They stood outside awhile, undecided, with their luggage, bags, and purses, and looked back at the darkness of their homes. Often, they acted as though they had forgotten something and returned to their houses; however, there were some who lowered their heads as we had and did not even return a second glance.

Complicating matters was a heavy snowstorm that swept over all of East Prussia between January 22 and 26, which only increased the despair. The storm left mountains of snow on the streets — something we had not seen in this part of the country in a very long time. Under any other circumstances, the cutting cold would have driven each and every creature to seek protection indoors. Instead, the streets were covered with massive backups of wagons, people, and animals, all of whom could only advance slowly.

The storm did not last, but an improvement in the weather was hardly a blessing. As soon as the snow clouds lightened up, little Soviet fighter planes entered the scene, growing in numbers each day. The aerial attacks joined the cold and the exhaustion as threats to us trekkers. Those who died along the way — old people, sick people, children, and anyone hit by a Soviet strike — remained in the streets where they fell. The rest continued on, walking like shadows.

My family was part of these shadows. Mother, Grandmother, my 14-year-old brother, Detlef, my 7-year-old sister, and I kept walking. Like everyone around us, we all carried backpacks with whatever was most valuable to us.

Valuable! For a moment I forgot all about the contents of my backpack seeing all the other people. Valuable! I really wondered what mother would think was valuable for me, probably two shirts, my Sunday pants, a sweater from my father, and at least 10 handkerchiefs. Valuable! She still did not know that I had chosen to pack the items dearest to me: a blouse and a skirt that I had taken from her some three years ago. They were more valuable to me than the 10 handkerchiefs, which I would not miss, not even if were attending church on Sunday.

In the early morning fog the next day, it felt as though ghosts had made an appearance. They came out of every home and moved along without a sound. I could see the unfortunate people as if through the thick white-veiled curtain, all moving slowly, very slowly. We followed the ghostly movement and saw the first dead people at the side of the road. No one had the strength or time to entertain the thought of burying them.

At one point, a group of soldiers scattered in front of us and disappeared into a snow-filled ditch alongside the highway. A horse reared on its hind legs and tried to escape its harness. And then I heard it — the sound of an airplane was above us. I pulled my grandma, mother, brother, and sister to the ground along the side of the road.

We stayed down for a while and listened to the rattling sound of the bombers that circled above us. Would the planes strike us or move on? Then, after what seemed like forever, all was still once again. Even the breathing of the people seemed to be silent; the only sound was the quiet grinding of the horses' hooves against the icy ground.

Just as we thought we were safe, another airplane swooped in from the left, flying lower and lower until it started to shoot. There were screams. But then — as quickly as it had approached us — it passed us, pulled up, and, fortunately, did not return. No one was hurt, but the incident instilled a fear that remained deep in our bones.

The further we separated ourselves from our city — a beehive of soldiers, women, and children — the more often we saw horse-drawn wagons. Just last summer, they had transported the hay and grain from the fields to the barns. Now they had been converted to mobile homes. It must have been just like that, I thought, when the pioneers traveled through America in an effort to find new land: wagon following wagon, with roofs made of wood and reed or simply covered by blankets placed upon frames. The women and children sat inside on boxes while the men directed the horse from the front or walked alongside with a loaded shotgun, always ready.

But no, my imagination about the American West did not fit with the reality that I saw in January 1945. For one thing, we were fleeing rather than exploring new land. Even though the wagons were full of boxes, bedding, and children, and might have looked adventuresome to some, it was women who were at the front to guide the unkempt horses. There were no men along, at least none who could shoot. Men in uniform did not belong with the wagons. Anyone who could walk at all walked alongside the wagons in order to protect the strength of the animals. No one knew how long the animals, or they themselves, would have to endure.

In Dirschau, about 20 kilometers west of Marienburg and two days into our trip, my fur-lined gloves were stolen. Apparently, I had put them down somewhere and forgot to pick them back up. There was no point in trying to get another pair, but I couldn't bear to walk without gloves in the freezing weather. Only during the most unusual times does one's life depend on whether or not one has gloves. Since I had worn two pairs of socks, I put one pair on my hands, and they became my gloves.

We continued onward. In the distance, we saw the extensive line of people, all covering themselves as well as they possible could. It wasn't snowing that night, but the strong wind made walking difficult and the air twirled with previous days' snow. Things were especially hard for my maternal grandmother, 80 years old, who found it difficult to trudge through the snow.

The next morning, after we had trudged through the snow some six miles and found refuge in the barn on a farm, there were two disturbing discoveries. One, and most tragically, Grandma passed away from frost exposure in that barn. During the first light of day, I attempted to wake her so that we could continue on our trek westward. Following a few unsteady steps from her on the straw-covered floor, she collapsed. She made another feeble attempt to get up, and then I heard her say, "That is the end." She may have been ready to give up, but I wasn't. I gathered help. Some people first tried to carry her outside in an effort to load her onto one of the horse-drawn wagons. However, there was nothing they could do to save her, and she passed. We could not expect more help as she had died, and we could not ask others to carry a dead person. In the end, we simply had to leave her where she had laid on the hay and slept, while the rest of us moved on. There was no time or opportunity to bury her.

The second discovery was the result of Mother's demand to inspect what my siblings and I had each packed. To her utter surprise, she found my treasures, the blouse and the skirt. My secret had not lasted long. She dismissed them, saying they were not appropriate for a boy and, despite my tears, discarded them. Looking back now, after I have learned to accept myself many years later, I found it significant that in an environment far from peaceful, I still needed to express my feminine nature. That blouse and skirt were my secret wardrobe for several years prior to their discovery and loss. No one encouraged me to wear those items. I felt they were more suited to me than the logs or toys at Christmas or other occasions.

Still, we had to keep walking. My pack was lighter without my blouse and skirt, although my heart ached with sorrow. Still, we had bigger problems. The thermometer was sinking further and — even worse — a strong east wind developed.

It was in these difficult conditions that we were blessed with a stroke of luck. We came upon a convoy of trucks that had stalled during an airplane alert. To illustrate priorities of the German military at this the time of chaos, we discovered that the two German soldiers were trying to rescue a truckload of coffee beans in 100-pound sacks. They considered this a worthy load. Mother began talking with the driver of the truck, and after a brief conversation, they took pity on our motley group and gave us permission to board the bed of the truck.

Our ride on the coffee truck came to an end after 40 kilometers, in the small town of Preussich Stargard. The two soldiers decide to turn north toward Danzig, while we wanted to continue west toward Berlin.

After a grateful farewell, we found the town's railroad station. The platforms were packed with people and luggage. Suddenly, there was a stirring among the crowd. A locomotive pulling some 15 cattle cars and a number of open flatbed cars slowly entered the station and came to a stop. Then we saw something that was gruesome, yet also saved our lives. The large doors of the cattle cars slid open. From each car, soldiers began to unload frozen dead bodies and pile them up against the terminal. The station looked like a ghastly army camp.

Adding to the apocalyptic feel, we suddenly heard the unmistakable sound of bombs. Everyone cried, "Airplanes! Airplanes!" The mass of humanity stormed across the tracks to the cover of the terminal. We were paralyzed by fear, but we had no choice other than to stay. There were about 50 other people besides us remaining on the platform. As the sound of airplanes faded away and the fear slowly subsided, we were able to board a boxcar and claim a far corner covered by a thin layer of straw. We were lucky to have been in the right place at the right time. The living now filled the cars that had, only several minutes earlier, been occupied by those who had died.

All of the cattle cars were haunted by a terrible smell. The only light came from a few petroleum lamps. In one corner of the car, there was a small iron stove, from which pipes stretched toward the roof. They were red-hot and smoking. We were sharing the car with 15 soldiers, who were laying on straw mats. They were all severely wounded. Next to the mats were buckets filled with the stinking sludge. From time to time, the wounded soldiers would moan and whimper under their thin, wool blankets. My mother felt ill and threw up.

The train headed westward. For three days, we had little to eat as the train continued its journey. When it stopped in the town of Schneidemühl, we stayed on the train while Mother ventured into town with a goal of finding some food. In the center of town, she came upon a commotion at a bakery. She discovered that the bakery had just baked several loaves of bread, and everyone nearby had converged on the scene, hoping to get something. Mother was always fierce, and she succeeded in buying two loaves before running back to the station as fast as she could. She nearly wasn't fast enough. As the station came into her sight, she could see the train slowly start to pull away. Now her only concern was getting back to us. Garnering all her remaining strength, she ran after the accelerating train when someone, alerted by her screams, pulled her into the last car. To me, these have always been God's hands that helped her. Had she not received assistance, I doubt that we would have ever seen her again.

Shortly after noon, we heard a siren. A few bombs fell in the nearby town and we developed a terrible fear that our escape may have been too late. Still, the fear passed and around 3 o'clock in the afternoon, the train continued onward. There appeared to be some draft of fresh air in the train, and the smell of blood, petroleum, and excrement became more bearable.

Still, the ride was not without commotion. I remember that the train suddenly stopped and stood for a long time as we heard shooting from a distant forest. It turned out that the locomotive didn't have enough water and the conductor uncoupled the locomotive from the cars to get water somewhere. There was nothing we could do; we simply stood and stood, hoping that he would return and we could continue with our journey. The sound of shouting came close and closer, and we realized that the attackers would reach the train. Finally, at the last moment, the locomotive returned and our voyage continued. When we arrived at the next city, we saw marks on the side of the engine where it had been hit.

Our journey continued, and we passed through a station in a town that had been completely set on fire. This must have shocked the locomotive driver, for he drove through the next two stations at high-speed. Only several towns later did he begin to pick up more refugees.

As we advanced westward, the train stopped periodically, which wasn't usually a cause for concern. After a few days, however, there came a stop that imbued all of us with a sense of dread. Whereas the previous stops had lasted only a few hours, this time the train had not moved for over eight hours. We were in the middle of nowhere, in the middle of a forest, with no city in sight. Having spent seven or eight days traveling by this point, we'd developed a certain instinct about what was to come. Every start up or sudden jerk had been a sign of hope, a chance to escape from the onrushing Russian troops and the atrocities they were committing. Every stop flattened these hopes. This time, our instinct said that something was terribly wrong. In the distance, we could hear the sounds of shooting.

As the hours passed without movement, one of the few men among some 80 women and children crowded into our cattle car, carefully pushed the door open to peer out and try to determine what might be the cause of the hours-long stop. As it turned out, we had been left on this track without a locomotive. Further investigation revealed that the engineer had uncou-

pled the three cattle cars packed with soldiers and had taken off. The locomotive had run low of water and the crew chose to lessen the load, which
meant leaving all of us behind. We were sitting ducks and the sound of
gunfire was creeping ever nearer from the forest.

It was now early morning, bitter cold, and light snow was falling. We stood
frozen in place, knowing that soon our attackers would reach the train.
The gunshots grew louder and louder. With each detonation, we huddled
closer to Mother in a corner of the cattle car; while the stench of human
waste was stronger away from the door, at least we got a little relief from
the wintry blast.

Before long, yells and screams accompanied the sound of shots. Suddenly,
the sliding door of our car was ripped open and several rounds of submachine gun were fired into the ceiling. What followed only confirmed our
fears. The Mongolian Soviet troops, clad in their gray uniforms and fur
caps, ordered everyone out of the rail cars and into a wide ditch between
the tracks and nearby cemetery wall. My brother and I were ripped from
my mother and sister as they segregated the men from the women. At first,
their hatred was aimed mainly at Germans in uniform. We watched in hor-
ror as several German soldiers were lined up against the cemetery wall and
executed.

Then it was our turn. In a stern, deep voice, they commanded my 14-year-
old brother and 12-year-old me to line up along that same wall where, just
minutes previously, we had watched the soldiers die. I was standing against
the wall; not far from me lay an older soldier who hadn't died from the shooting. He was on the ground, softly moaning due to his wounds. The Russian
soldiers raised their weapons, aiming them at us. They paused and broke out
into loud laughter. After a while, they herded us together and marched us to
a collection point. From there, trucks took us to a small village.

We did not want to look as we were taken away, but we could see Russian
soldiers dragging the women forcefully towards homes or barns. While
my brother, sister, and I ended up at a Soviet internment camp guarded
by Russians, Mother did not fare as well. Even though she tried to make

herself look less attractive and old by covering her hair with a babushka, the drunken Siberian soldiers herded all women, including my mother, into a nearby home where she was repeatedly raped.

"GU TTE, go to GU TTE, go to go to GU TTE," were the sounds that Mother heard as the Russians attempts to command in very poor German. She felt the tightening grip of the fist on her arm. "Frau house HOUSE."

She tried to resist. But a tight Russian grip pulled her into the nearby house. She fought, tried to pull away, but she had to see the wide, pock-scarred face that belonged to the fists. She smelled the stench of whiskey and sweat that came from the face and saw, with a quick desperate look, that other women had been thrown into the snow, with plump figures in Russian military uniforms lying on them.

The soldiers weren't shy about using force. They pressed submachine guns or knives to the chests of those screaming. Mother saw a pregnant woman wrestle with one of the men in the gray-brown attire. He tore her fur coat apart, pulled a straw bundle from the barn, and forced her onto it. She cried hopelessly, half suffocated, and knew in that moment why so many of the soldiers had been holding knives to women's hearts.

This sexual violence was an extension of the barbarity that had defined the conflict on the Eastern Front. Some Soviet soldiers saw it as a time to pay back what the Germans had done to Soviet citizens with destructive looting and rape. They had been given absolute freedom to seek revenge by ravaging and plundering and did not hesitate to take full advantage of desperate civilian refugees in a situation like this. Historians estimate that perhaps 2 million German women were raped by Soviet soldiers at the end of World War II and during the postwar period. For decades, no one talked about the sexual violence. Despite medical records, women in Communist East Germany after the war were sometimes forced to sign statements saying that, officially, they were never raped.[4] In the soon-to-be-founded

---

4. Westervelt, 2009

German Democratic Republic, the Soviets were to be thought of only as liberators, and liberators did not commit war crimes.

Political fear mixed with shame and guilt about the atrocities committed by Nazis led to a kind of code of silence about these events. Those raped did not speak about what happened to them. Nobody talked about that the damage; the danger was too great. Only in recent years have people begun to talk. The efforts have been led in part by Dr. Philipp Kuwert, a psychiatrist at the University of Greifswal. Talking about how Germans suffered at the end of the war is complicated. It does not minimize or erase the monstrous crimes of the Nazi regime, but at the same time, the pain of German woman deserves acknowledgment.

Mother was gang raped by five Mongolian Russians. The memories of her experience would come back repeatedly. Sometimes after she talked about it, she would sleep for a few hours and then wake up crying. It was impossible to forget.

After the night we were separated, Mother ultimately arrived at the same internment camp as Detlef, Marianne, and me, and we were able to reunite. Over the next few weeks, we were put to work for the Russians. Equipped with shovels, picks, or wheelbarrows, we were employed to repair the grenade and bomb craters that were impeding traffic to the front.

It was the dead of winter, and nightfall came early, around 5 p.m. One evening, as our workday neared its end, my mother, brother, sister, and I hid in a culvert under the highway as the work crews were gathered to march back toward camp. Once they had left, we sprung from our hiding place and walked toward the west and the front lines. Our journey took several days. We would hide in the thick of the forest during the day, moving only at night. And then, suddenly, we found ourselves in a section of Germany that had not yet been taken by the Russians. After everything that had happened, we were safe; it seemed like a miracle.

As was the practice at the time, the Red Cross stations were identifiable by signs behind the front lines to help the swath of refugees coming in from the east. The Red Cross was a true lifesaver for so many of us refugees. For example, they provided housing for my aunt, Tante Josie, who fled on her own, by horse drawn wagon after my Uncle Paul was drafted into the German army.

The Red Cross provided my mother, siblings, and me with transport to Berlin, where we arrived in the middle of an air attack. Following the all clear signal, we were sent to Potsdam and quartered in an apartment vacated by a political Nazi family who had fled to the west. The city had many huge tenement buildings, usually covering all four sides of an entire city block.

Potsdam was a change from the places I had known before. The city blocks were lined with huge tenement buildings. Potsdam also offered me a very special treasure: a bicycle. This bicycle was not like those of today. It was a baker's bicycle, the three-wheeled kind that bakeshop owners or their apprentices would use to deliver bread or buns in the early hours of the morning. The back end of the bike supported a large box to carry the bakery products. Obviously, these bikes have long been obsolete, as bakers rarely deliver their wares anymore.

I was lucky to find such a bike in Sanssouci Park, a beautiful park in Potsdam on the grounds of the estate of the former German Emperor Frederick the Great. The bicycle was in decent shape, except that the steel rims were devoid of tires. Nonetheless, I did not let this trivial matter stop me from inaugurating the first baker's bike transportation system for our new neighborhood. My brother and I had a lot of fun offering box transportation to the small kids of the apartment complex. Admittedly, the ride was a little rough and noisy, but no one seemed to mind.

Of course, our stay in Potsdam was not all fun and games. In the same park where I found the bicycle, so close to where we lived, we saw about 20 bodies of dead Germans soldiers following a day of bitter fighting. I was disgusted when I realized that some of the teenagers would desecrate the bodies by stealing the watches and wallets of the dead.

Even in Potsdam, we were not safe from the war. The British Royal Air Force (RAF) targeted the city, especially its industrial center and railroad facilities, in order to weaken the Germans. By this point in the war, the German air defense was considerably weak. Only a few German JU 88 planes were available to counterattack the RAF, which had hundreds of bombers. Since the Germans couldn't compete with the British in the air, we had to do what we could on the ground to protect ourselves. When the alert sounded, we would cover our doors and windows so that no light could escape into the streets. The blackouts supposedly made it more difficult for the British planes to find their target.

While we considered the blackouts a nuisance, we felt the real effects of the war due to the food rationing system. The German government was determined to keep the country fighting as long as possible, and this meant preserving the limited food we had through a Spartan-inspired diet. The system was so unwieldy that the people of Potsdam joked that even those who managed to survive the war would be driven mad trying to figure out how to legally eat. Each person received seven different ration cards every month, each a different color: blue for meat; yellow for fats, cheese, and dairy products; white for sugar, jam, and marmalade; green for eggs; orange for bread; purple for nuts and fruit; and pink for flour, rice, cereal, tea, and coffee substitutes. We had long since run out of real coffee, so it was made from barley and acorns.

During the early years of the war, most people did get enough to eat, but supplies deteriorated as the conflict progressed. Toward the end of 1944, food supply had become a real problem, and it was not unusual to stand in line for nearly 24 hours to get a pound of horse meat per person.

Hunger leads people to take extreme measures. One day, we heard that several large barges on the canal leading from Potsdam to Berlin had burned and were smoldering on the water. Mother, Detlef, my brother, and I rushed to the scene to retrieve what we could. Using a rope, my mother dropped my brother and me into the smoking barge. As we clung tightly to the rope, she lowered a bucket on another rope and we began scooping rice into it. Our plan might have gone perfectly, except at that moment, we heard the unmistakable sound of Russian fighter planes approaching. Mother, recognizing the noise, managed to crouch behind a cement pylon on the side of the canal, while Detlef and I luckily avoided the bullets that hit the ship. Then, as soon as the two propeller planes appeared, they were gone. Mother pulled us back up, and the bucket of rice lasted our family a long time.

This was not our only devious method of obtaining food. We found some hidden treasures right inside our apartment building. Each tenant had a compartmentalized storage unit, and my siblings and I discovered one day by peeking through the gaps that some people were hanging salami or sausage in the storage space. We figured out how to sneak into the units and greedily consumed our bounty in the park.

Despite our adventures, the final year of World War II was a time of unimaginable pain and suffering in Germany, and it was only a matter of time before Potsdam would be hit. April 14, 1945 was my mother's birthday, but it was hardly a day of celebration. Instead, we could see the obvious sign that a major air raid was coming. The skies were filling with spots shaped like Christmas trees, as some 500 Allied Lancaster bombers took an unopposed run on Potsdam. Their goal, supposedly, was to soften up this city for the ground troops.

Our three-story apartment building at the outskirts of Potsdam near the Sanssouci Park had an air raid shelter. Following the sirens, our building's 68 inhabitants found refuge there. Never had I experienced such rumble and noise. Suddenly, a large bomb hit our building, collapsing the structure above us into a cloud of dust and rubble. Even in the fortified air raid shelter, we were showered with cement and debris. While my mother, brother, sister, and I managed to escape serious injury, our neighbors on the south end of the building were not so lucky. Of the 68 tenants in the shelter, exactly half were pulled out still alive two days later. The other 34 perished.

When we emerged, Potsdam was a ghost of the city it had been just a few days earlier. Official statistics say that around 5,000 Germans died that night.[5] Another 25,000 evacuated the city because of the threat, and many of them never returned.

Our family, however, had nowhere else to go for the time being, so we stayed in Potsdam. The Red Cross found us an apartment building that had survived the bombing relatively unscathed. My brother and I found a beautiful, deserted mahogany kayak that we used freely on the beautiful Lake Wansee, located between Berlin and Potsdam. On occasion, we might bump into a submerged object only to discover that it was a body of a deceased person. It was a common occurrence.

On another occasion, we found several sets of German military field telephones in the park. With our neighborhood friends, we set them up in order to connect our homes. However, this was a concern for the adults — several other tenants came to see my mother and pled us to get rid of the phones. They were concerned that the incoming Russians would assume we were spies and punish us all. As you can imagine, the phones were soon gone.

Luckily for us, the war was coming to an end. One day, we heard shooting in the park behind our new home. As the sound grew closer and closer, we gathered in the air raid shelter downstairs, but that did not hide us from the front-line Russians soldiers who came storming through the door of the basement and fired warning shots into the ceiling. They searched the room for any military men; fortunately, there were none with us. Then, they asked for something to drink. My quick-thinking brother clapped a Russian soldier on the shoulder and took him to our kitchen to give him a glass of water. The thought of it still makes me laugh.

A few months after the war ended, a notable historical event took place in Potsdam. From July 17 until August 2, the three most powerful leaders in the post-war world — Harry S. Truman, Winston Churchill, and Josef Stalin, the heads of government from the United States, Great Britain, and the Soviet Union, respectively — came together to discuss the future

---

5. Clodfelter, 2017

of Europe. The conference took place in Ceciliendorf, a palace built three decades earlier for German Crown Prince, Wilhelm von Hohenzollern.

These world leaders, collectively known as the "Big Three," were debating the very future of the land where I grew up. Germany had been sandwiched at the end of the war, with the Allies coming in from the west and the Russians from the east. Although millions of Germans had fled during the last months of the war, many were now trying to return.

Stalin wanted to expand Poland, which was under Soviet control, to the Oder and Western Neisse rivers in East Germany. He argued that no Germans lived in this territory anymore, as they had all fled. The Western Allies finally agreed to the land transfer, which eventually led to the creation of East Germany. The Prussians whose families had lived there for centuries had no say.

Of course, my brother and I were not going to let such a monumental historical event take place nearby without trying to get a peek. While we weren't privy to any of the workings of the conference, we went to Ceciliendorf and saw Churchill, Truman, and Stalin enter their villa from their automobiles.

My brother had always been a very independent individual. One day, we discovered that his schoolbooks were deposited in our kayak, stored inside the basement hallway of our building. He had temporarily left us to make the journey some 400 kilometers to our native East Prussia and try to determine what was left of our estate. While he was there, a Polish person shot him through his thigh. After about three months, he returned to Potsdam and would reunite with the rest of our family later on.

The end of the war also gave us the chance to reunite with our father. He was a very brave officer. It is a miracle that he survived the war.

Towards the end of the war, his unit was driven into a close circle near the city of Heiligenbeil at the southern coast of the Frische Haff, an inland lake known as the Vistula Lagoon in English. It is a large lake, about 80 miles in length but only four miles in width. On the northwestern end of the lake lies the Frische Nehrung, a peninsula that separates the lake from the Baltic Sea. My father and his troops were on the other side of the lake, and their only refuge was to swim its width and reach the peninsula. My father, fearless as always, commanded his unit to swim four miles to the Frische Nehrung, even though there was a layer of ice still in the water. Clinging to a barn door, he swam to the peninsula where he resumed his command.

On May 3, 1945, five days prior to the end of combat activities in Germany, my father was wounded — for the 13th time during the war — by shrapnel while showing another officer into position. Ironically, this injury saved his life.

At the time, there were only a few small boats remaining to offer rescue from the onrushing Russian troops; appropriately, they were reserved for severely wounded soldiers only. My father was carried onto one such vessel on a stretcher. Their little minesweeping vessel sailed westward on the Baltic Sea, and my father was taken prisoner by British troops off the coast of Denmark. By this time, the war had come to an end, as Germany surrendered on May 8. My father was treated very well in his prisoner of war camp and was soon released to a relative who lived near Frankfurt in the American sector of Germany.

When the rest of our family had arrived in Potsdam at the end of February, my mother had sent my father a number of postcards on the front informing him of our location. He'd held onto that information throughout the rest of the war, and now all of his efforts were devoted to finding a way to make contact with us.

However, communication was not easy during the postwar period, particularly between the Allied-controlled western Germany, which included Frankfurt, and the Russian-controlled east, which included Potsdam. My father received a lucky break in the form of an advertisement: the American army was looking for drivers to bring many dozens of trucks from West Germany to Berlin, only 30 kilometers from where the rest of our family was residing. At the time, Berlin was a pocket of Allied-controlled territory inside Soviet-controlled East Germany, and the trucks were to be used for the logistical support of the American-occupied zone of the city. Following their arrival, my father and the other drivers were interred at a school while they awaited the transport back to West Germany.

The note we received was short, but said everything we needed to know:

> I am in Berlin. Being retained by US troops. Please come immediately, location: Johan Wolfgang von Goethe Gymnasium, Linden Strasse 92.

It is truly amazing that this cryptic note was delivered to us at our apartment in Potsdam, 30 kilometers from my father's location. It was particularly remarkable because there was a tight curfew between the hours of 8 p.m. and 6 a.m. during this time. My father should not have been able to communicate with the outside world while he was interred at that school, but he managed to beg a local passerby to deliver the message. From the goodness of his heart, an elderly gentleman, who had caught my father's attention when he happened to be passing by the school, rode his bike from Berlin to Potsdam to deliver this all-important message. We were very grateful.

The note was the first sign of life from my father since we had fled East Prussia in early January. At that time, we had known only that father was alive and fighting on the Frische Nehrung. Mother immediately made plans for our trip to Berlin. A neighbor offered to take care of my 7-year-old sister. I made sure that there was enough air in the tires of my latest bicycle, which I had confiscated when a Russian occupier parked it outside of a building. Detlef was still in East Prussia in search of what was left of our home.

In the early morning following the receipt of Father's message, Mother and I embarked on our 30 kilometer trip to Berlin. My mother sat on the horizontal bar of my bike as I, the 12-year-old, peddled. Luckily for us, the highways were deserted, as Germans had neither cars nor gasoline at the end of the war. This allowed us to take the Autobahn.

The trip was far from pleasant. I had developed a case of dysentery, which forced me to run for the ditch along the highway many times, and the hard pedaling only elevated my fever. But despite my agony, we reached our destination around noon. It was a dramatic reunion. We had doubted we would ever see our father again and had feared that he might be in Berlin to be turned over to the Russians.

Now that we were reunited, Father obtained permission from the American officer in charge for our whole family to accompany the group of three trucks back to Frankfurt in a few days' time. My mother and I left quickly to return to Potsdam before the 8 p.m. curfew. We had to pack for our trip. As Detlef had not yet returned from his venture to East Prussia, we informed a neighbor of our plans, and they promised to notify him when he returned to Potsdam.

By noon on the following day, our bicycle caravan left our temporary home in Potsdam for Berlin. Once again, Mother occupied the bar of the front of the bike. My sister sat between the two cardboard boxes, which contained all our worldly possessions, on the two-wheeled trailer I had found in the park and rehabilitated and hooked to the saddle of the bike. I was pedaling a little harder than the previous time, but driven by sheer willpower, we reached our father at 7:45 p.m.

We thought that we would have a simple trip to Frankfurt, but our plans did not materialize. The American officer who had previously given us permission to accompany our father on the trip west now changed his mind and withdrew his OK; Father was supposed to return to Frankfurt without us. However, he and the other drivers were determined to figure out a solution. During the night, they loaded the bike and trailer onto the truck that would take some of the drivers back and hid us under some tarps. About 7 a.m., they boarded and the convoy of three trucks departed Berlin. After about four hours and 200 kilometers, the trucks came to a stop and the drivers disembarked for lunch. We remained hidden under the tarps and everyone boarded again. They whispered to us that this was our last stop before reaching the border between East and West Germany.

Suddenly, a pair of hands belonging to a U.S. soldier lifted the tarp, exposed us, and ordered us off the truck. Someone had squealed, and they had found us. We had no choice but to disembark. Father and our worldly goods moved on with the trucks, while Mother, my sister, and I were left standing by the side of the road.

Our situation — a mother and two children abandoned in the middle of nowhere — was complicated by the tense political situation in post-war Germany. We were somewhere in the Russian-controlled territory of East Germany; we estimated that we were about halfway between Berlin and the border. We had only one thought in mind: continue our trek west and catch up with Father. We set out for the border town of Helmstedt, which we reached a week later. Along the way, we dodged several Russian patrols, subsisting mostly on sugar beets and raw potatoes that we stole from the fields.

Arriving at the border was only the first part; we now had to cross. The Cold War between Russia and the Allies had already begun, which meant that the border between East and West Germany was highly controlled. Many were apprehended or shot while trying to cross. Those who were caught were often thrown into informal camps not far from the border, guarded by Russian soldiers.

The situation had a special niche for locals who used their knowledge to work as guides, helping others escape across the border. Mother, my sister, and I sought their help. On one occasion, our guide assembled a group of about 30 people in a patch of rye that was bundled and stacked up prior to its transport to the barn. We huddled against the stacks as the guide made the rounds to collect his fee. The actual border was about thousand meters to the west. Suddenly, there were searchlights all around us. Russian soldiers, with their submachine guns drawn, rounded us up and herded us back to one of the camps. On three other occasions, we were caught by patrols and returned. On the fifth attempt, we finally succeeded.

That night was lit by a full moon. We were lying in a row of potato plants, contemplating our next move, when three men appeared out of the dark.

They were walking at a fast pace towards the border. All three wore the former German Army uniform. They weren't happy to see us, repeatedly asserting that they had no use for a woman with her kids, but we tagged along after them anyway. I remember wading through a swampy area, a creek bed where Mother lost one of her shoes, and up a steep embankment. And then we crossed the border and arrived in West Germany, closer to our father.

We embraced the three former German soldiers who, despite their objections, had guided us toward our target. In total, our journey had been over 200 kilometers since the convoy of trucks had abandoned us, but we finally made it. Now that we were in West Germany, we made our way towards Niedershausen to find my father. That journey was long too, though on occasion, a driver of a passenger car took pity on us and gave us a lift, considerably shortening our trek. About three weeks after we had initially been separated, we finally arrived in Niedershausen. My father had been making arrangements to look for us, but it didn't matter now. At last we were together again.

With help from the Red Cross, which was tasked with helping displaced Germans, my father had managed to find a room in the small village of Niedershausen, located northwest of Frankfurt. Upon our arrival there, we wrote to an old neighbor in Potsdam with our new address. When my brother Detlef returned to Potsdam from his excursion to East Prussia, our neighbor informed him of our move, and he was able to join us in Niedershausen not long thereafter. Our family of five lived in a small room that belonged to one of the village families. The room was equipped with a potbelly stove, which was used to cook our meals and heat the room. We all slept on straw mats and found ways to survive.

To provide firewood to last us for a year, the local government assigned us a large beach nut tree, approximately six feet in circumference, in a forest several miles from our place of lodging. This tree kept me busy for several months. With a borrowed saw, my father and I cut it down. Next, we trimmed the small branches and cut the larger branches into segments about four feet long. We stacked the pieces neatly until we could transport them to our temporary home. Our widowed neighbor was kind enough to loan us her wagon and cows for the multiple trips that were necessary to bring all the cut logs to our house. It was about a four-mile trek, but that wasn't even the hardest part. Every day, when I didn't have to help our neighbor tend to the fields, I would use wedges to split the four-foot logs into more manageable size. Then I would use a regular bow saw to saw each piece into length of approximately 14 inches. This took several weeks. Next, using a butcher block, I would ax the 14-inch pieces into even smaller pieces, about 4 inches in diameter. Finally, after all the wood was chopped into the small pieces, I piled them into a sort of giant igloo with an approximate 10-foot circumference wall. The rest of the pieces were thrown into the center. It provided us with sufficient firewood to last all winter.

We also began to raise animals. With my woodworking abilities, I was delegated to build several stables using scrap pieces of wood I found. The front entry was equipped with mesh wire that provided light and air for several chickens, who routinely provided us with fresh eggs. I also took charge of a small herd of rabbits who had found their way into mother's pots.

I vividly remember a major tragedy involving the little rabbits. One pair of these beautiful animals had given birth to six babies, which I treasured until an accident ended their life. One night, a female neighbor meant well when she fed our little bunnies late one evening. Unfortunately, she was unaware of their feeding habits. The climate in Niedershausen was usually pleasant during the day, and dewy and frozen at night. Our dear neighbor left some extra cabbage in the rabbits' enclosure, where it found itself subject to some frost, but the rabbits still ate it. Apparently the frozen cabbage then expanded in their little stomachs, and all the babies died.

As food was scarce, we collected whatever we could. In the forest, we could gather beechnuts and convert them to oil at an oil mill. We also collected mushrooms and sold them to grocery stores. I also gained a sort-of employment with our widowed neighbor. Her husband had died fighting in

Russia, and she was left controlling about 200 acres of farmland, as well as two cows. I helped her out with farm chores in exchange for daily meals.

I started going to school again, which made for a bit of a hectic schedule. Every morning at 4 a.m., I would go to her barn and milk the two cows. Niedershausen was located about six miles from the city of Weilburg, where the nearest school was located. The school, Gymnasium Phillipinum, had existed for many decades and was located in the center of Weilburg. I had to take the public bus there and back each day. In class, I found the discipline to be very strict. I also began to learn English, a skill that would serve me well later on.

When my classes were finished for the day, I would return to Niedershausen and continue to help on the farm. I would use the cows to tow a wagon and some equipment out into the field to complete whatever was needed that day — usually plowing, cultivating, or raking. The reward was a good meal at dinnertime. I was 13 years old at the time.

Also living in Niedershausen were my Uncle Erich and his family, who were quartered in a room at a farmhouse similar to ours. Uncle Erich had three children, including my 15 year-old cousin, Eberhard, who shared my first and last name.

Food was always scarce, and the men and boys of our family began participating in wild boar hunts. Following the disarmament of all Germans at the defeat of World War II, these creatures had considerably multiplied and were causing damage to farmers' fields. At the request of the government of Niedershausen, the American army provided a platoon of about 20 men to thin out this heard of boars, usually on a weekly basis. If a boar was killed, we were rewarded with a large piece of meat. This would be the only meat we would taste until the next successful hunt. We weren't always successful, but it was worth a try.

Prior to each hunt, the army gave the hunters a very specific set of instructions. The U.S. Army men would be positioned at 500-meter intervals around an area of forest extending two kilometers in width and three kilometers in length. We walked the length of the forest in a straight line, hoping to route the boars and chase them toward the shooters. For safety purposes, the Army men were always very clear: never shoot into the direction of the patch of woods through which the German drivers were moving. Shoot at a boar only once they have run out of the woods and away from the shooter.

One drizzly morning that I will never forget, my cousin Eberhard and I once again responded to a call for help with the boar hunt. As our motley group lined up at the edge of the forest of beechnut trees, I told Eberhard my wish: "I hope we'll have more luck today."

It seemed we would. We were trekking for the forest when I heard the unmistakable BANG, BANG, BANG, the sound of a carbine firing. A splintering of tree branches and the thud of bullets hitting the tree right in front of me followed almost simultaneously.

I had temporarily lost sight of Eberhard, so I yelled out to him: "Be careful, a boar has been wounded!" On our last hunt, an injured 200-pound boar had charged at us, forcing us to find refuge up a tree, and I was hoping to avoid a repeat of that situation.

The shooting had stopped just as sudden as it began, I carefully peered around the big beechnut tree that had shielded me seconds earlier. Then a gurgling sound caught my attention. A bright red blood stream led toward the edge of the woods from where the shots had originated. As I crept closer, I could make out the source of the gurgling. It was Eberhard, who had crawled some 15 meters and collapsed. A bullet had entered his left shoulder and severed his carotid artery in his neck. We later determined that a second bullet had penetrated his left leg.

There was no chance to save his life. Within 10 minutes of the shooting, he had bled to death.

There was so much irony wrapped up in my cousin's death. The two of us, named identically, had survived the horrors of war, only for him to die from friendly fire during a boar hunt. It just as easily could have been me, but I was left alive — left to carry the name Eberhard onward.

Chapter 3
New Homes, New Family

Until our unexpected reunion in Berlin in early 1946, I didn't really know my father. By then, I was 13 years old, and he had been away fighting since 1939. Well, who was he?

Earlier, I mentioned that my father was the 14th and youngest child in a rather well-to-do farm family. His father had been the typical autocratic strong head of a large farm and flour mill. In the tradition of old Germany, the oldest child usually inherited the management of the property while all other siblings either married, got an education and, most commonly, a job elsewhere. For instance, my mother, who was one of seven children of another prosperous farm, was sent to France at age 18 for one year, for the purpose of gaining the kind of mannerisms and education that were typical for a child of a rich family.

My father, in turn, became the beneficiary of the so-called Treaty of Versailles, signed between the Allies and Germany after World War I in 1919. One of the major results of this treaty was that Germany, having been defeated in World War I, was authorized to form an army of 100,000 men. My dad enlisted into the new army late in the 1920s for a period of 12 years. At the time of my birth in 1933, he had achieved the rank of sergeant.

When Germany declared war on Poland in 1939, he held the rank of lieutenant. He was immediately involved in combat in Poland. During this time, our family lived in the town of Elgenau, very close to the Polish border. During the entire time of his enlistment, he lived on post with his unit, while the rest of our family was in a nearby town. Thus, he spent little time devoted to raising his three children. That was Mother's job.

When the war expanded to include the Western Allies and the Russians, Mother and we three kids had moved to Marienburg, West Prussia, from where we eventually fled the marauding Russians.

In conclusion, my father was pretty much a stranger to us when we got the news that he was located in Berlin Zehlendorf, awaiting transport back to the American occupied part of Germany. Although I had visited him a few times at military bases and once on the front lines, we had not actually lived together in a very long time.

Despite our limited relationship with our father during my early childhood, my siblings and I were full of anticipation when we learned of his location in Berlin. When we finally were reunited, we saw him, really for the first time, in civilian clothes, as a man who had aged quite a bit. It was a tearful embrace as he welcomed us at the school building where he was detained.

We learned that he had received several battlefield promotions to his rank of major. He told us that he had sustained 13 war wounds — equivalent to 13 Purple Hearts in the U.S. Army — and received many decorations, including the Iron Cross First Class and the coveted Close Combat Medal for his 32 eye-to-eye close combats. He was purely a soldier; he never had any political ambitions.

After our family's time in Niedershausen, we moved to the larger city of Weilburg and found a nice apartment on Limburger Strasse — quite the upgrade from the single room our family had shared for a year and a half. I continued attending the Gymnasium Phillipinum for the next four years, now with a shorter commute.

Stronger evidence of my female thought process became apparent during my teenage years. I recall, for instance, dressing in some of Mother's items I had stolen away, with a scarf wrapped around my head, and walking right past my very best male friend without being detected. I got a real kick out of that.

Most of the time, though, my desire for femininity was something I had to push aside. I held onto some of my Mother's clothes, keeping them hidden in my cabinet drawer. When I was alone, I would try on some of her lipstick, but that was all. Mother never mentioned that blouse and skirt that she had caught me with when we were escaping.

In Weilburg, we tried to establish a normal family life. One of my father's first jobs was a dishwasher in an American Caserne. The U.S. Army maintained a substantial presence in Germany after the war, and someone had to wash the dishes in the barracks. Unfortunately, his job there ended when he was arrested and jailed for two months as punishment for stealing food. His only motivation for stealing was that our family often went to bed hungry.

Although he was ultimately caught, I must say that my father's methods were quite ingenious. A farmer near the U.S. barracks had permission to pick up the garbage, such as potato peels, from the kitchen where he washed the dishes, in order to feed his pigs. Father convinced the farmer to be his accomplice; my father would place some leftover food, such as pancakes, at the bottom of the garbage cans, add some cardboard on top of the food, and then put the potato peels and the other garbage at the very top. The farmer would pick up all of it, and then we would go to the farmers' barn to pick up the leftover food. It was a nice additional source of nourishment while it lasted.

Later on, Father found employment with the German Customs Office. His job was to regulate small farm-based alcohol distilleries. He inspected all the distilleries and determined the taxes that each owed.

During a time of great scarcity, my father somehow managed to secure a soccer ball. At the time, it was the only ball in town. I had begun to play soccer while still in Niedershausen at age 13. When we moved to Weilburg a year or so later, I played with the youth team. Since I was the only one who possessed a soccer ball, I allowed the adult team to use it at the pitch right along the Lahn River. Often times, the game was interrupted when someone accidentally kicked the ball into the river and it had to be retrieved before the game could proceed. To this day, it amazes me to see nets full of balls at the U.S. training sites or games.

My father, the brave soldier he was, experienced depression after losing both the war and his career as a German soldier. To compensate, he developed a habit of smoking and drinking excessively. His weekly job lasted from Monday morning until Saturday at noon. After work on Saturday, he would frequently go to a particular pub, play the German game of *skat* (similar to bridge) with three or four other buddies, and drink a lot of Schnapps, always ending up very drunk.

Sunday mornings, while the other townspeople would walk to church, mother would send me across town to the pub to help dad to walk home. These Sunday mornings were among the most humiliating moments of my life. Dad would sway as he walked and try to accost the passerby. For me, the experience was a lesson. Never would anyone experience me drunk or smoking. I was so ashamed.

Despite his limitations, my father was very caring toward Mother and us. He died at 76 from the long-term effects of his many war wounds. Unfortunately, my lifelong contact with him would be very limited.

At the age of 20, I moved from Weilburg to the much larger city of Frankfurt. All of my soccer training had paid off, as I had received an offer to join the major league soccer team Eintracht Frankfurt. I also hoped to complete my education and find a supporting job. In those days, a soccer career with the so-called Bundesliga, or First Division, did not reflect the kind of income that players receive nowadays. While today soccer stars from all over the world play in the Bundesliga, the team was made up entirely of German nationals when I played. Because playing soccer wasn't a career with which one could support oneself in 1954, players on such teams derived a portion of their income from jobs outside of soccer.

I found housing in a youth home in the Frankfurt suburb of Schwanheim and began working on the side as an intern at an overcoat manufacturer called Petrykofsky and Fritz. To commute to my place of work in downtown Frankfurt, I took the public streetcar, Line 21. As it turned out, this particular streetcar line was also the daily mode of transportation to work for a pretty young woman named Ruth. It did not take long for us to strike up a friendly relationship on Line 21, and one event soon led to another.

Each day, I packed myself a rye bread and herring sandwich for lunch. Ruth noticed my rather barren pickings and took pity on me. She began to pack an extra lunch, which was always much tastier than what I would have made myself. After we had known each other a little while, I learned that her birthday was approaching and her parents had scheduled a party for her. It took all my diplomatic skills to gain an invitation to the event. At her day of honor, I arrived with a bouquet of flowers for her mother and asked her for the first dance. From that day on, I was a frequent guest at their house, and before too long, we were engaged to be married.

A year after meeting Ruth, I left Petrikofsky and Fritz and found employment as an interpreter at a Frankfurt department store. The store was located in the downtown area near the city's major hotels and attracted many American tourists. The English skills I had acquired during my time at Gymnasium turned out to be very useful.

One day, I was attending to an elderly American couple from Cleveland, Ohio in the department store when they asked about my background. I mentioned my interest in everything American and told them that I was hoping to someday live in the United States. In response, my customer inquired why I hadn't considered immigration.

The thought of immigration had certainly crossed my mind before then, but it had never seemed practical. American immigration laws at the time made it difficult to immigrate to the United States without a sponsor, and I did not know anyone there. My engagement to Ruth also complicated matters. I explained these problems to my customer, but he was not deterred. Instead, he explained that he owned a manufacturing company in Cleveland, Ohio, and offered to sponsor me and employ me as a salesman. He said that Ruth would be able to come along too. This appeared to be the stroke of luck that we would finally need to fulfill my dream and was another argument to Ruth's parents that she and I should finally get married.

Convincing our parents to let us move to America was another battle. When Ruth and I had first met on the streetcar between Schwanheim and downtown Frankfurt, she was only 19 while I was 21. When our dream of immigration to the faraway land of America began to seem like a reality, and we were genuinely discussing the details of planning our trip, our parents — especially Ruth's — tried their best to dissuade us from a joint departure. They argued that I should first immigrate by myself and after I had found employment and housing, have Ruth follow.

Ruth and I did not want to be separated, much less be on different continents. After several months, during which we were waiting for our visa, we convinced our families to let us immigrate. We held a beautiful wedding at an old church in Schwanheim. As a married couple, we would be able to have a single visa issued in our joint name.

Shortly after our wedding, Ruth was awarded the title of Certified Seamstress Journeyman, which would come in handy after our American immigration. We were still awaiting our visa, so our first home in Frankfurt was a converted goat stall. It was so small that our bed had to be folded up during the day. We did not have running water, and the only toilet was an outhouse in the back of the property. But the home was our own, and we were very happy there.

Ruth and I were still awaiting our visa, so we embarked on a traditional honeymoon trip. Our vacation was adventuresome more than luxurious, but it was one I will always remember. We had a small pup tent and made plans to tour the south of Germany and parts of Switzerland and Austria over the course of two weeks. The countryside scenery was beautiful and, in the high elevation of the Alps, we woke several times in the morning to find fresh snow covering our pup tent. For our travel purposes, my father loaned us a nice looking 500 CC BMW motorcycle with a sidecar. I had never driven the bike before. By today's standards, a 500 CC is not a powerful motorcycle, but it was very exciting at the time.

Anyone who has driven on the highways in Switzerland and Austria knows that often the roads are cut into the sides of mountains, with drop-offs of hundreds or even thousands of feet. The roads are narrow — much narrower than in the United States — and at times during our trip, the wheel of our sidecar would be just inches away from sudden death. Poor Ruth! All she could do was remain seated in the sidecar and pray that we would not fall to a grisly death.

One particularly treacherous moment nearly cost us our lives. We were motoring along on a two-lane highway, following a slow-moving truck and trailer, and I thought that the highway conditions would allow me to pass the truck and increase our speed a bit. Unfortunately, I had not realized that what appeared to be a long straightaway, which would give us sufficient time to pass, was actually a curve that I had not anticipated. Traffic was fast approaching from the opposite direction and, despite full power, it became questionable whether we would be able to complete our pass prior to a frontal collision. I raised my left hand in an attempt to warn the oncoming traffic, all the while willing the motorcycle to go as fast as it possibly could. At any rate, we barely cut in front of the truck being overtaken. It was a close call, and a valuable lesson for the rest of our trip, and we returned safely from our honeymoon, ready for our upcoming American adventure.

The actual application for our immigration visa took more than a year in total. In the interim, my career playing professional soccer improved greatly. We moved out of our refurbished goat stall and into a nice apartment with a sloping roof. We furnished it as well as we could and life was good. Of course, our early marriage couldn't pass without some challenges.

Ruth fell ill and a hospital visit revealed that she required emergency appendectomy. After the surgery, she left our home for a two-week recovery stay at a German sanatorium.

And then it happened. While Ruth was away to regain her health, I received the notification that our immigration visa was finally available. I quickly sold the little furniture we had, bought two one-way tickets from Pan American Airlines and, when Ruth returned, confronted her with the fact that on next Wednesday we were scheduled to fly from Frankfurt to New York by way of Gander Newfoundland. We had never flown before and, I must admit, when our DC-7 just kept rolling during its takeoff roll, I was very anxious. We had exactly $64 in our pockets when we arrived in America.

We had left behind our families, our apartment, our jobs, and everything that we really knew. What attracted us to the great United States?

In 1954, nine years after the disastrous World War II, Germany was still struggling economically. At the same time, the country was receiving a strong dose of American culture. The U.S. government wanted to introduce a democratic lifestyle to the defeated Germans — perhaps in part to make sure that we would not fall under the communist ideology that the Soviet Union was pushing on our neighbors to the east. One tool in this plan was the screening of American movies, featuring stars such as Elizabeth Taylor and Burt Lancaster.

I admired feminine, glamorous woman like Taylor and had a strong desire to be just like them. Woman like this were not visible in German society, and I hoped that, in America, I would be able to emulate their makeup and lifestyle.

My personal desires aside, we were also attracted to America thanks to the works of prolific German author Karl May. Although May was a German writer who never went further west than Buffalo, New York, he set most of his book in the American West

His books, set in America, focused primarily on two characters: Winnetou and Old Shatterhand. Winnetou was the young chief of the Apache tribe; Shatterhand, the author's alter ego, was a German engineer who traveled west to help with the railroad development. Shatterhand promises to look after Winnetou, and the two men form a great friendship in spite of their different backgrounds.

When Shatterhand first arrives in America, he is described as a greenhorn, with very limited knowledge of the Wild West. Still, he has his strength — both physical and moral. Shatterhand can knock someone out with one punch, and sustained only bruises when he fought grizzly bears with a knife. Because he is fresh from abroad and in possession of ancient Teutonic values, Shatterhand is honest and moral, untainted by the ways of the greedy white man. He is like Superman and Lone Ranger all rolled into one. He is the ultimate immigrant success story.

Shatterhand represented a mindset and a way of thinking that inspired many Germans. He fit in and succeeded against the odds without sacrificing the person he was. We could only hope to achieve something similar — although perhaps without punching grizzlies. But it wouldn't happen so easily. Following our long-anticipated arrival in America, our dream would experience a rude awakening.

After we arrived safely at the Idlewild Airport in New York, we retrieved the single suitcase and cardboard box that held all of our belongings and met a driver in a black Cadillac whom our sponsor had sent to New York to pick us up. The driver took us through Harlem and we got our first impression of the United States. Our luxurious trip in this impressive car ended many hours later at our sponsors' 18-room mansion in Cleveland Heights, Ohio.

Unfortunately, any idealized image of America that we developed during this initial car ride was quickly shattered by the realities of our new immigrant life. Instead of the sale's job that our sponsor had promised me, we were informed that we would first have to show our appreciation for his generous sponsorship. Ruth replaced the maid that our sponsors' had previously employed to tend to their house. This was ironic because back in

Germany, Ruth's family had employed a housekeeper themselves. Instead of employment in sales, I became our sponsors' handyman. Prior to our arrival, our sponsor had rented us a basement apartment and furnished it with furniture from the Salvation Army. For the furniture, we were told we owed $2,000. Jointly, Ruth and I were paid $50 per week for our indentured service.

Prior to our departure from Germany, our parents had warned us that we would ultimately beg them for money to return to Frankfurt. But even though our start in America was not quite what we envisioned, we would not give up so easily.

Ruth commuted by bus from our small apartment to our sponsors' home in suburban Cleveland each day. She did not speak or understand English, so she struggled to communicate with people. I taught her to say "no" whenever a strange man talked to her. Of course, this meant that a seatmate might want to say something perfectly friendly, like "Is it not a beautiful today?" and she would still respond with a fervent ,"NO!"

The salvation for our language difficulties came from a lovely couple and a very wonderful story. One afternoon, Ruth was trying to communicate with our apartment building's janitor, but could not do so, as she still spoke very little English. At that moment, another woman walked by and asked Ruth what languages she spoke. That woman, Rosalie Bronner, spoke German and several other languages, and became my wife's immediate translator, as well as our closest friend.

Rosalie and her husband Kurt were originally from Budapest, Hungary. They had survived Auschwitz, one of the most infamous Nazi concentration camps during World War II, while all of their immediate family had been murdered by the Germans. To this day, Rosalie and Kurt have their numbers from the concentration camp tattoo on their arms. They became our angels and lifesavers.

Since Ruth and I did not own a car at that time, Rosalie would take us along on joint shopping trips for groceries and the like. Once, Rosalie and

Ruth bought a little Christmas tree in a pot for us. Ruth suggested that we should also buy one for them — little did we know that Jews do not celebrate Christmas.

Rosalie and Kurt still live in Encino, California, and we remain very good friends. I recently visited them with my daughter, Maureen, with the specific intent to thank them for their love and help during some 60 years. They receive our ultimate adorations, as they repeatedly went out of their way to help us — even though our fellow Germans had brutally murdered their entire family. They had a beautiful baby daughter, whom they named Eve, who has now grown up. Rosalie and Kurt are now in their early 90s. They are still wonderful company after all these years.

While Ruth and I had found great friends, our work situation was not nearly as enjoyable. Our sponsor showed no sign of giving us the work we had been promised. When I asked him in a pleasant, businesslike manner when I might expect the job he had offered to me back in Germany, he became very nasty, and we left our indentured service. I continued to pay off the $2,000 debt for our Salvation Army furniture, and he left us alone.

My father, whom I discussed at length at the beginning of this chapter, never visited Ruth and me in the United States. Later in life, I was fortunate to visit my parents often, as I traveled to Europe and took up temporary residency in Geneva and Brussels. Although my father and I had little in common, it turned out that I would follow his penchant for military service — mine just happened to be for a different country.

Chapter 4
Serving the Country

After our acrimonious separation from our sponsor, Ruth found a job at a Highbees department store, where her former training as a seamstress was very useful for their alteration department. Every morning, I accompanied Ruth to her job in order to interpret her assignments for the day. Not long after, I found employment there myself in the men's suits department. I was working in my new job one day when I struck up a casual conversation with a part-time colleague. His regular job was with the Allegheny Ludlum Steel Corporation, the largest producer of stainless steel, electrical steel, and elevated temperature alloys that are used in the jet engine industry. As it happened, the company's sales department was looking to hire someone. I applied and got the job.

The steel sales job was much more pleasant than my time with our sponsor; unfortunately, it was cut short after just a few months. Even though I was a German citizen and had been in the United States for only 10 months, I was notified, that as a legal immigrant, I was being drafted into the U.S. Army. It turned out that, legally, an immigrant was eligible for the draft if his immigration documents indicated that U.S. citizenship was his goal. Since I hoped to become a U.S. citizen someday, I was eligible for the draft. I would eventually become a citizen, but only after completing three years of service in the Army.

My time in the Army began with eight weeks of basic training in Fort Carson, Colorado. A few days into basic training, the drill sergeant asked our squad if anyone had any prior military service. I raised my right hand, and was named acting squad leader for basic training — a position that could result in better duties. I received an official armband, and I am pleased to say that my squad excelled in all disciplines. The sergeant never asked what my previous military training was, which was probably a good thing. The answer would have been Hitler Youth.

When I moved to Fort Carson for basic training, Ruth had to stay behind in Cleveland. Being alone was not easy, as she lived by herself and her English skills were still limited. So when she received my first postcard, she became desperate to see me. She took a leave of absence from work and hitchhiked all the way from Ohio to Colorado. When she showed up at the post guesthouse demanding to see me, the men on duty informed her that they were there to train the recruits, and family visits were not possible. Ruth, however, did not take no for an answer, and the officer on duty ultimately relented and issued me a weekend pass, allowing me to leave the base and spend time with my wife. We had a lovely weekend that resulted in something wonderful: Ruth became pregnant with our first daughter, Maureen.

Once my training was complete, the Army assigned me to 18 months' duty in Germany. It was a perfect location, only 40 miles from my parents' home. Ruth was able to join me thanks to help from her parents, and Maureen was born on November 19, 1957 at the American hospital in Heidelberg. Coincidentally, it is the same military hospital where General George S. Patton died. As my active military duty made it impossible for me to be a present father initially, Maureen spent long periods of time with Ruth's parents at the beginning. I was home every night, but my in-laws simply adored Maureen and — since we were only 40 miles apart — they begged for the opportunity to take care of her.

I was assigned to a tank battalion in Mannheim, Germany with a military occupational specialty (MOS) as an ordinance parts specialist in the motor pool. However, my language skills turned out to be much more important than my skills with machines, and the army used me mostly as an interpreter.

The army was hardly glamorous. We went from New York Harbor to the German port of Bremerhaven by boat. While I have always dreamed of being on a cruise, the voyage across the Atlantic on the troopship SS Buckner was not the trip I had dreamed of. There were approximately 500 GIs on board, and my hammock, five stories below deck, was nothing like a vacation room with a balcony that I had imagined in my vacation dreams.

Soon after my arrival in Germany, I bought a 1949 Buick from a sergeant who was returning to the United States after completing his assignment. I paid $350. The car was in excellent condition, except that it consumed a lot of oil. However, since I had been assigned to the company motor pool, oil supply was never an issue.

My military duties were fairly basic. The army used me primarily as an interpreter to resolve court material cases or maneuver damage claims. As an interpreter in court, I was instructed to repeat all testimony verbatim, and some cases could be rather uncomfortable. For example, I sometimes was the translator for German woman alleging rape by American soldiers, and I often felt very self-conscious when interpreting: "The soldier tore off my dress, my panties, and my bra." But I had to follow instructions.

My own female inclinations had very little role in my life during this time. Germans are inherently very obedient and the U.S. Army only magnified this quality; I always followed the orders from above. As such, my circumstances prevented any sort of female expression. I didn't dare keep female clothes with me as I had as a child.

Overall, my tour of duty was very pleasant. While some people took issue with the draft, I considered it as my ticket of admission to beautiful America and ultimately citizenship.

Being in the army was not all work; we tried to find time for entertaining pursuits as well. Prior to my immigration to the United States, I had played professional soccer for a German team. This fact came to the attention of my company commander, who asked me to form a team from our company's personnel. In 1956, soccer wasn't terribly popular in America, and there were very few GIs who had much background — just a few guys from St. Louis and Chicago who had played soccer in high school. Our team was composed of many immigrants like me, but to outsiders, we seemed like a motley bunch.

Nevertheless, our company team challenged the U.S. Army All-Star Team to a friendly Friday night game followed by dinner and beer. The All-Stars had a perfect record prior to the game. But that would change — my team beat them by a score of 7 to 0. Eventually, after a couple of beers, we admitted that of the 11 players on our team, nine had previously been German semi-pros. In fact, some of them were members of a team that I had played against on weekends back when I played for Eintracht Frankfurt.

My German heritage and language abilities gifted me many advantages while serving in the army. About once a month, our company staged field maneuvers. In the field, the troops were fed from the field kitchens, and the menu left much to be desired. I had the advantage of being mobile with a jeep assigned to me, and I was able to communicate with nearby German innkeepers, who frequently maintained a small restaurant on their farms at out-of-the-way locations. We had an arrangement that, when we beeped the horn of the jeep twice, the barn door would swing open, and we would proceed to enjoy a great German meal.

While the army officially used me as a court translator, sometimes many of our negotiations were not very official. In one typical example, our tanks took positions in some unknown fields along the Rhine River, only to sink deep into swampy soil. The unit's tank retrievers sank up to the top of their tracks too, and thus were unable to pull our tanks out. It fell upon me to bribe the local rail crossing keepers to let us "borrow" a truckload of ties that neatly stacked up, awaiting rail replacement. The bribe was easy — it usually took just a carton or two of cigarettes. There was only one problem: the railroad ties "disappeared" under the load of the tanks, never to be retrieved, and a legal claim followed.

After Ruth joined me, we found a small apartment in the city of Wein-heim, about six miles from my base in Mannheim. I would frequently take the streetcar to and from my post. In my U.S. Army uniform, I would sometimes overhear unflattering remarks from a German passenger. To their surprise, I would respond in their local dialect. The reactions were quite funny.

My time in Germany was not entirely limited to army work. After several months on assignment, Ruth and I took a vacation to Italy and the French Riviera in our Buick. We were equipped with a small pup tent and other gear. At the time, the price of gasoline from the PX was just 10 cents a gallon. We filled up 10 five-gallon cans of gasoline and loaded the car with our other supplies. The Buick was weighed down heavily — our license plate just about hit the road surface — but we had everything we could possibly need.

On one occasion, we camped at the beach of San Remo, Italy, directly across the very snooty casino where players were seen entering and leaving in their elegant dress. That evening, rain threatened our little pup tent, and Ruth secured our wallet in our car nearby. The next morning, we left the campsite for a day trip to Monte Carlo, about 49 miles away. Before we reached our destination, I asked Ruth to double check that she had our passports and wallets. We discovered that during the preceding night, someone had stolen them.

Rather than complete our trip, we were required to return to our tent in the campsite, where word of our situation quickly spread. We informed our friends that we were now forced to immediately return to Germany, as we had no money. We called our parents to ask for financial assistance and were repacking our car for the disappointing return to Germany when a delegation representing some 250 tents approached us. They offered us an envelope containing about $350 in currency from some 15 nations — representing about the same amount that had been stolen. They hoped that this would allow us to stay longer, and we did. It was a beautiful reflection of international friendship.

I credit my success in the army to the strength of my German upbringing, especially my father's military career. I served for two years in Mannheim, and at the conclusion of my assignment to Germany, was awarded the title of Soldier of the Year in my division and honored with a parade. Afterwards, I returned to the United States and served one more year with a Reserve Stevedore Company in Cleveland, Ohio. My time in the army taught me discipline, obedience, and how to cooperate with others. Not long after I was discharged, I finally became a U.S. citizen.

Eberhard, Marianne (sister), and Detlef (brother); the boys are in Hitler Youth uniform

Major Benno Burchert (father) in 1944

Eberhard on scooter in 1935

Detlef, Paula (mother), Marianne,
and Eberhard around 1944

Castle at Marienburg, founded in approximately 1300

Eberhard passport photo from 1958

Eberhard attending Quarter Master School of Army in 1956 in Virginia

A general congratulates Eberhard as Soldier of the Year during parade in his honor

Eve in 2003

Eve in her home in 2010

Eve in 1995

Carole in 2009

Carole, Eve, and Mitzi in their home, Christmas 2000

Caitlyn Jenner, Maureen Burchert (daughter), and Eve at College of Marion County

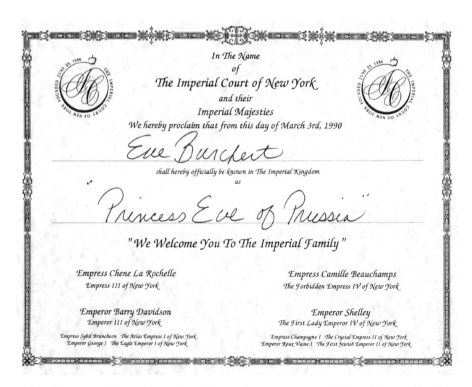

In The Name
of
The Imperial Court of New York
and their
Imperial Majesties
We hereby proclaim that from this day of March 3rd, 1990

Eve Burchert

shall hereby officially be known in The Imperial Kingdom
as

Princess Eve of Prussia

" We Welcome You To The Imperial Family "

Empress Chene La Rochelle
Empress III of New York

Empress Camille Beauchamps
The Forbidden Empress IV of New York

Emperor Barry Davidson
Emperor III of New York

Emperor Shelley
The First Lady Emperor IV of New York

Empress Sybil Bruncheon The Atlas Empress I of New York
Emperor George I The Eagle Emperor I of New York

Empress Champagne I The Crystal Empress II of New York
Emperor Roux Vaine I The First Jewish Emperor II of New York

Certificate awarded at World of a Thousand Gowns event at Waldorf Astoria Hotel,
New York; sponsored by New York Gay Community

Eve in 2017

Chapter 5
Geneva, Charm School, and the End of My First Marriage

My 25 years of marriage to Ruth were very turbulent. We were happy to have two beautiful daughters come into our life, and we devoted much of our attention and love to their upbringing. My career advancement offered us a good life.

Following my military service, I returned to my employment with the steel company, Allegheny Ludlum. After working for a year as a sales correspondent at the District Office in Cleveland, Ohio, I was chosen, along with five other candidates out of hundreds of applicants, for advancement through the corporation's six-month executive training program in Pittsburgh. My family stayed in Cleveland while I commuted occasionally between Cleveland and the corporate headquarters in Pittsburgh. The training covered all phases of salesmanship and the details of all of the company's steel manufacturing mills and research lab. After completing the program, we were all assigned to various district offices as salesmen. I had the exceptionally good fortune to be assigned to the company's newly formed export department. It was the perfect job.

At first, I was based in Pittsburgh, Pennsylvania, and our family moved there for two years. I was frequently away from my family, as I traveled extensively across Europe and to countries such as Australia, New Zealand, India, Pakistan, and Mexico to develop sales of the company's specialty steel. Then I was assigned for two years to Geneva, Switzerland to help establish the European sales network. Ruth joined me in Geneva, while our daughter Maureen stayed with Ruth's parents in Frankfurt. This period was followed by a one-year stay in Brussels, Belgium, where I coordinated the sales network of a newly formed joint venture called Allegheny Long-doz. Ruth again joined me in Brussels, and we rented an apartment in the suburbs. After Belgium, I returned to Pittsburgh and was appointed the company's export manager. Not long after, our second daughter, Renee, was born.

My career advancement provided numerous exciting opportunities. Allegheny Ludlum produced stainless steel; electrical steel for motors, generators, and distributors; and high temperature alloys used by manufacturers of turbine blades and buckets in jet engines. Every year, we exhibited the high temperature alloys at the Paris Air Show at Le Bourge Airport. I would stay at one of the best hotels in Paris, the George V, each summer. In 1969, I had the great pleasure to meet the Apollo 9 astronauts, James McDivitt, David Scott, and Rusty Schweickart, who had just returned from space and were send to Paris as the American ambassadors to the Air Show. I accompanied them to the famous Lido Night Club and to the villa of Robert Sargent and Eunice Shriver Jr., the American ambassadors to France at the time. The Shrivers were members of the Kennedy Family, and it was a huge honor. Maria Shriver, who is now a famous television reporter, was 9 years old at the time

Several years later, I was asked to assume the position of Vice President of Sales for a newly acquired subsidiary in Chicago, Illinois. This company served to sell and distribute electrical steel through just-in-time programs to manufacturers of transformers, motors, generators, and laminations. To accommodate my new job, our family of four moved to Chicago.

To an outsider, my life seemed typical. Two decades after Ruth and I had arrived in New York with $64 in our pockets, we seemed to be living the American dream. We were married with two beautiful children; I had a steady job. But our home life was not so simple.

My desire to be a woman had simmered inside me since I was 7 years old. But a particular finding pushed this desire from an unspeakable fantasy to a palpable possibility: the story of Christine Jorgensen. Christine was born as George Jorgensen. George had been drafted into the U.S. Army in 1945, but had undergone a series of sex reassignment operations in Denmark in the early 1950s to become Christine. She picked her new name after the Danish doctor who had completed her surgeries, Dr. Christian Hamburger. As I read her story — how she sought release from a male body that had always felt foreign to her — I could immediately relate. Until that day, my transgender thoughts had always been an absolute secret to my wife, but in a single moment, the dam broke.

It was a beautiful summer weekend in Geneva when I confessed to Ruth my innermost fantasy. I had a limited wardrobe of female clothing at the time, and I insisted that she see me dressed as a woman. It was the first time I had dared to cross-dress during my adult life.

Whatever I had hoped Ruth's reaction to my secret would be, the effect on our marriage was disastrous. That same day I showed her part of who I was, she declared her wish to divorce me. However, such a separation was not so simple. We had money to think about and daughters to raise. For the next 18 years, her threat of a divorce remained just that.

Still, with my secret out to my wife, I began to think about my alternate persona. My given name, Eberhard, would not fit for a woman. Instead, I chose the name Eve. Any similarity to my birth name is purely coincidental, although it has come in useful to have the same first letter for computer usernames and the like. Rather, I thought of Eve as the first woman mentioned with Adam. It was also the name of the daughter of Rosalie and Kurt, my first American friends, so it seemed appropriate for me. I like the name. It says it all.

Later on, I found an article by the transgender activist Dr. Virginia Prince entitled "166 Men in Dresses." The article, which ran in a magazine called *Sexology*, discussed the topic of "transvestism," a term used at the time to

refer to cross dressers and transgender people.[6] As I read this, I again re-
membered my own love of female clothing. It was another reminder that
there were people out in the world who were like me.

While I began to develop my transgender identity, our family life continued. My career in the steel industry advanced; our daughters grew up. One
of the most pleasant periods of time that I remember took place in North
Barrington, Illinois, a far western suburb of Chicago, about one hour by
commuter train ride from downtown. During the time we lived there, it
was home to many executives, and the neighboring Barrington Hills had
many horse farms. We lived in a section of North Barrington called Biltmore. My employer underwrote my membership in the old country club. I
played a lot of golf and tennis and sailed on the exclusive lake.

I did start to dress as Eve and experiment with makeup, but in secret
from my family. While I began to meet up with other transgender people
through groups and at conferences, I remained simply Eberhard with my
wife and daughters.

Our family initially lived in a townhouse. It was here that Maureen, my
older daughter, found out about Eve for the first time. The year was 1973
and she was 15 years old. Maureen had noticed the tension between Ruth
and me; when I greeted Ruth after coming home from work, she would
push me away. Maureen later told me that she thought her mother was
being mean and felt sorry for me, so she decided to do some detective
work. In my closet, she found dresses hanging and a number of wigs in
round boxes. She thought they must belong to Ruth, but she was confused
because Ruth did not wear wigs.

Then, in the center drawer, she found pictures of Eve in an envelope. When
we discussed the event recently, Maureen told me that she was initially
taken aback but also felt a sense of relief, as she had solved the mystery of
what was going on in her parents' marriage. A few days later, she told Ruth
what she had found when the two were out shopping. She said that Ruth

6. Prince, 1962

became so distraught that she had to pull the car over to the side of the road. When they arrived home, Ruth told me what had happened.

When I asked Maureen how she felt about her discovery, she said that now it all made sense. She didn't have a problem with me being Eve; the knowledge explained more about who I was to her and why I was away so much. However, she wanted me to tell Renee so that she would not have to discover it on her own. Ruth and I both agreed that we couldn't do that. Renee was too young, just 10 years old at the time. We asked Maureen to keep the secret until her sister was old enough to understand.

Maureen also encouraged us to get a divorce, saying that we shouldn't stay in a marriage where we were clearly unhappy for her and Renee's sake. We told her to mind her own business.

It was not until five years later that we decided to tell Renee, at that point 15 years old, the truth. Maureen was home from college and we all went out to dinner at a nice restaurant. As we sat around the table with food in front of us, Ruth and I jointly told Renee who Eve was. She reacted with shock and stormed out of the restaurant. Ruth ran after her while I quickly called for the check. Eventually we all headed home, and Renee never wanted to talk about it.

Many years later, as Renee and I have begun to discuss our relationship, I have been told that I was not a very doting dad. I saw us as a typical busy corporate family where everybody sort of went their own way. The girls entered high school; I traveled a lot on business, played a lot of golf and, while I loved them dearly, it is quite possible that I was guilty of not giving them the attention they needed at the time.

My relationship with Ruth can be summarized as an uneasy coexistence of two young people, trying to keep the marriage alive. It was all a big lie. To others and to ourselves, we pretended to be happy, yet, deep down, neither one of us was. Still, we were both very afraid to let our immediate family know the extent of our unhappiness. Our sex life, while never very enterprising, became virtually nonexistent. During the long period of 18 years between my coming out to Ruth and our ultimate divorce, we tended to more and more go our own ways. I met people who shared my gender fantasies, while Ruth developed her own circle of friends.

Through my friends, I learned of the possibility to attend a charm school for transgender people in Gleneden Beach, Oregon. It was a week long course, the length of a vacation. When I informed Ruth of my plans, she told me that — if I decided to head west for charm school — I would find my possessions on the lawn outside our condo. It was not a bitter end: she promised that she would assist me in locating an apartment and give me basic supply of dishes, furniture, and other necessities. Thus, the day I had long expected but mentally resisted had finally come. I formally signed up for charm school, and Ruth declared that she was initiating divorce proceedings.

And so, 25 years of marriage ended. My children were 15 and 19 years old at the time. Maureen was a freshman at the University of Virginia while Renee was still in high school. Their reactions from the beginning were very different. Maureen was generally accepting of me, while things were more difficult with Renee. I realize that the situation, even independent of my transgenderism, would have been harder for her, as she experienced the divorce while still living at home.

For me, Ruth's decision was in many ways an utter relief. The extended period of peaceful but unproductive marriage proved very stressful and frustrating, and I simply did not have enough courage to break things off on my own. Thus, I traveled to Oregon for charm school with a spirit of adventure and a weight off my shoulders, looking toward the new horizons that lay in front of me.

The trip required meticulous preparation and planning. Prior to my departure, I received a letter from the organizing committee with precise instructions for my arrival. When I reached the airport in Portland, Oregon, there would be someone with the designated task of meeting the arriving attendees. Having never met before, we would identify him by a smile button on his jacket, which was given to all attendees and organizers. As I left for the trip, I fastened my smile button to my jacket. Waiting for my departure from the gate in Chicago, I scanned the terminal to see if any other men were wearing one too, but I didn't see anyone.

I had better luck in Portland. Upon disembarking from my flight, I quickly located my newfound friend with our matching buttons. We drove approximately two hours to Gleneden Beach in his pickup truck.

The organizing committee secured an entire block of condos, each of which would be occupied by two attendees. This was the place where my fortunes would change entirely. In my condo, I could transform myself into Eve. I could not wait to disrobe out of my male clothing, take a shower, and apply makeup, which I had practiced oh-so-secretly at home many times. I put on my first outfit, which I had planned in advance and rehearsed at home. Then I ventured outside. I was amazed by how comfortable I felt in such an environment; surrounded by people like me and those who were accepting of us.

Charm school was a quite novel concept. The idea to offer modeling school classes to transgender people and cross-dressers came from a collaboration between transgender attorney Marilyn Irwing and modeling school director Gloria LaVonne. In the early 1970s, Ms. LaVonne had been invited to give a lecture on charm and beauty to a group of transgender individuals at a party in Portland, Oregon. At the time, she was not too familiar with transgender issues, but she enjoyed speaking about feminine beauty and the questions many of those attending had. At the party, she realized how much these interested people needed help. Their clothes were attractive, their wigs were combed but not styled, and they needed a lot of help in body language and makeup. Ms. LaVonne suggested to Marilyn how wonderful it would be to offer a condensed beauty and charm course. And so began the birth of charm school, the week long fantasy on the Oregon Coast.

The first program took place in 1973 and was called "Dream," as it was the deepest dream of every attendee to learn to adopt the mannerism of a woman. When I attended in 1978, the program was in its fourth session. Attendees came from all over the world — Canada, Malaysia, and the like.

Members of the staff of the Gloria LaVonne's modeling school led the classes at charm school. They were tasked with teaching us feminine mannerisms: how to walk, sit, apply makeup, get in and out of a car, and smoke a cigarette, all like a woman. Each night, the modeling staff provided a last minute check to assure the perfect look for the evening activities. I suppose it was presumptuous to assume that anyone could acquire feminine mannerism in a week long class after spending the whole of our lives learning the opposite, but we all hoped for the best.

Our time at the charm school quickly flew by. We had classes in the morning and the evening, interspersed by parties and fashion shows. We did learn a lot. At the culmination of the program, I was awarded the title of Miss Dream, named after the program's motto. It was truly the experience of a lifetime. My time at Dream propelled me into accepting Eve fully, and I have never looked back. That week was breathtaking and enriching; in retrospect, I only wish that more transgender woman had been granted the opportunity.

One of the 16 ladies from Gloria LaVonne's Portland, Oregon Modeling School was named Ruby Edwards. At the end of the course, she wrote and dedicated the following poem to me:

Me and Eve

There's a girl that lives inside of me
who keeps begging to be free.
When I was young she used to cry
and in confusion, I would sigh
and say, "Be quiet, go away!"
yet she begged, day after day.
Then as I grew, I somehow knew
that on some future day
that little girl would have her way.

So slowly, I let her come outside
— one quick shy look, then she'd run and hide
inside of me and safe again —
she begged to be set free again.
As I grew, she also grew and thru the years
we lived and felt each other's fears.

I wondered the, "How could this be
to have this woman inside of me
who wanted so much to dress in style
in beautiful things and all the while
I was a man in a man's world.
How could I also be a girl?
What twist of fate created me
when neither man nor woman could be free.
So, I named her Eve and dressed her well;
even my mirror couldn't tell
As she learned to use her female charm
she became both beautiful and warm
and I loved both parts each self could play
until, finally, I reached the day when I could truly say,
"I'm glad Eve finally had her way!"

Charm school was a truly one-of-a-kind experience. I realize that times have changed and that the "clandestine" behavior has fortunately given way to a much more open and accepting society. This is great; it is what we strived for. And yet, I often wish that our community of today could benefit from the experience that was Dream. It would be hard to duplicate this experience today. People no longer want to be kept in relative isolation, subjected day-long intensive trainings. And yet, I would not have missed it for the world.

Perhaps most importantly, charm school led me to a women who changed my life. Her name was Carole.

Chapter 6

Carole

ove at first sight is real. I know, because it is what happened to me when I met Carole.

When I left for charm school in Oregon, I hardly seemed to be in a position to start a new relationship. 18 years after I had confessed my innermost secret to Ruth and she had expressed her desire to divorce me, we had finally separated. Charm school was my chance to fully express my transgenderism — and, it turned out, was the place where I would meet the love of my life.

On my first day of charm school, I prepared and decorated myself the best I possibly could. Bursting with anticipation, I took one final look in the mirror and ventured out of my condo. In that moment, I got a little help from fate. The first people I encountered were two beautiful women. They introduced themselves as staff members of Gloria LaVonne's Modeling School who had been hired to teach attendees the female mannerisms that we greatly desired. They were Ruby — the woman who wrote me the poem from last chapter — and a lovely woman named Carole.

In retrospect, Carole awoke in me the kind of reaction that I can only refer to as instantaneous combustion. From the moment I saw her, there was an immediate feeling of affection that would never leave me throughout my

36 years of marriage to this beautiful woman. At the time, I expressed this feeling the way I always had, through a typical male comment: "Whoa, the help is certainly getting to look better all the time."

Charm school, where I was learning to act like a woman, would seem to most people like an odd place to meet my second wife. One may wonder how someone like me, basically transgender, could react such a way to Carole. My upbringing was always guided by the belief that every man should be matched with a woman. Even following my divorce, the thought of a single life never occurred to me. This may not be typical for other trans people, but I needed a companion. I could not help but feel that Carole was the woman for me.

During those seven days of basic woman training, there were signs that Carole shared my feelings of affection. We had support from her colleagues, who let me know that she liked me. When I returned to my condo one night, I found a fresh green apple on the pillow of my bed, a symbolic sign from Carole: "An apple for Eve." Before charm school was up, we exchanged addresses and phone numbers.

Because of the nature of our meeting, Carole knew I was transgender from the very beginning. I would later find out that she had never met or known a transgender person prior to that week, but she had trusted Ms. Lavonne's assurances that these men were safe and signed up for the seven-day experiment.

I further learned that Carole had recently separated from her husband, moving out of the home that she had shared with him and their daughters and into a small apartment of her own. In some ways, our lives were remarkably similar. We had both married young — she straight out of high school — and we each had two beautiful daughters. Carole's marriage was not a happy one either. Her husband had a drinking problem, several affairs and was generally abusive. She lived for her two daughters and her successful modeling job. She had no phone of her own, and frequently used a phone booth near her apartment to call me.

Carole was a prominent member of the Portland, Oregon Model Organization. She had a great career as a runway model and had gone on to perform in many commercials. She had begun teaching professional modeling at Gloria LaVonne's agency — mostly instructing professional models, although she also helped with events like charm school. Carole was attractive in every sense of the word. She had a pleasant personality, a wonderful figure, and was an excellent cook.

It quickly became clear that Carole and I wanted much more than our long-distance phone calls. About four weeks after charm school, I sent her a round-trip airline ticket from Portland, Oregon, to Chicago O'Hare. I anxiously counted the days until her visit. She was able to take a one-week leave of absence from her modeling jobs to make the trip.

As our individual marriages had left much to be desired, we were both ready for a memorable week enjoying one another's company. We took advantage of the many excellent restaurants in downtown Chicago and visited the theatre. She met several of my close friends. On one occasion, a business associate of mine invited us to his farm north of the city, where he maintained over 400 Lippizaner horses and treated us to a performance by his cadre of riders, all of whom had previously been employed by the Viennese Riding Academy. Incidentally, this herd of white stallions was descended from about 12 such horses that General George S. Patton had rescued from Russian ownership at the end of World War II.

Of course, more important than any outing that week was the time that Carole and I spent enjoying our newly discovered love. We were both starved for human contact and affection. The week passed far too quickly. While I was sad to see Carole go, we agreed that our separation would be temporary. Our feelings were far too strong for distance to keep us apart.

A month after Carole returned to Portland, I flew there myself. We loaded a few of Carole's possessions into her car and set out for Chicago to begin our life together. During our long drive, we had ample time to get to know each other. One obvious topic of conversation was my gender identity. Carole was curious to fully understand who I really was and to what extent my transgenderism might grow. The truth was, even I did not totally know the answer at the time. I simply assured her that I loved her and would never embarrass her by revealing my true nature before family, friends, and others. Over the course of our lives together, I never did.

After moving in with me, Carole quickly found employment as an office manager at the Chicago Merchandize Mart at the district office of Georgian Carpets. About a year later, when my divorce from Ruth was finalized, Carole and I entered into our own marriage before a civil court judge. By that point, we had moved into a very nice ground floor apartment in downtown Chicago. We had a small wedding party with about 30 friends in attendance. Life could not have been better.

While my desire to express my transgender feelings continued throughout our marriage to Carole, I rejected outing myself fully. I did become active in the transgender community, which I will discuss in depth in the next chapter; however, I rejected the possibility of living as a woman in my day-to-day life. I repeatedly turned down an offer from a well-known surgeon friend who routinely performed sex reassignment surgeries. He had offered me a big discount on the surgery should I decide to go that route, but there were just too many reasons not to.

Carole and I had a wonderful life together. If I had come out publicly as a woman, it would have turned her life upside down all over again. The political climate with regard to transgenderism in the 1970s and 1980s was poor; a drastic move like sex reassignment surgery would have had major consequences. I had a rewarding career in the steel industry and over of a decade of membership at a country club. We were not ready to give all of that up.

Carole's modeling career continued to grow in Chicago. She joined a prominent modeling group based in Barrington, Illinois and frequently modeled for up to 1,000 ladies at conventions in major Chicago hotels. She had a very active career and was genuinely in demand until the age of 65, which was exceedingly rare in her field. I admired her in every respect and often assisted her modeling activities by taking videos of her shows. On a few occasions, when the commentator for a fashion show was absent, I helped out by donning my tuxedo and leading the models through their entertaining show. I loved being right in the middle of the event.

Carole quickly ingratiated herself into my social circles, most notably at the Biltmore Country Club. One of my favorite stories to this day remains that of the club's annual stage production. Every fall, the club put on a stage production. Usually, they would hold two performances, each attended by about 200 people. I thought that involving Carole in the annual performance seemed like a good way to endear her into the club's social environment. One year, we attended the show together and, the next, we decided to attend the casting call. There seemed to be no suitable role for me, so I went home early without Carole. When she returned, she told me that the club would be performing "Cabaret," and she had signed up to be one of the chorus girls. She revealed that there were not enough chorus girls and a fellow good-looking male member, Rudy, was asked to play one of the girls. When I heard this, I immediately asked her why she hadn't volunteered me. She said she didn't know I'd be interested. The following day, however, I ran into the lady choreographer at the gas station and — after a small conversation — I was drafted to be a chorus girl. I wore a garter, corset, stockings, high heels, and a flowing blonde wig. It was the greatest fun I ever had. Many of the men in the audience with whom I played a lot of golf wanted to know who the tall blonde in the chorus line was. I never told them it was me.

My two marriages could not have been more different. Carole and I were true partners; we supported one another in every way. There is a German proverb that says, "If you want more knowledge, marry your teacher." In many ways, I did just that. Carole and I had many things in common. We would discuss fashion, makeup, and relate in some ways like two girlfriends to one another. We both had very good taste; from her, I learned female comportment. Sometimes I was Eberhard in these conversations; sometimes I was Eve. Either way, she loved and accepted me.

In fairness to Ruth, she had not learned of my deep-seated feminine identity until we had already been married for seven years. The news came as an absolute shock to her, and she was never able accept it. By contrast, Carole knew of my transgender tendencies from the moment we met. In me, she found a soft-spoken individual who treated her with utmost courtesy and respect. It was an obvious contrast to her previous life with a man who brought her only extreme disloyalty and abuse.

Our 36 years of marriage were based upon deep love, affection, honesty, loyalty, and mutual respect for one another. While my marriage to Ruth had been devoid of hugs and kisses, the opposite was true between Carole and me. There was never a day when the expression of our love for one another was not evident.

There was one missing ingredient to my marriage with Carole. Eventually, as the years passed, my use of estrogen — a female hormone that is often prescribed to transgender individuals — took its toll; our initially wonderful sex diminished totally. In my conscience, this was the only negative aspect of our relationship. I feel bad, to this day, that I deprived Carole of the sexual relationship she deserved. Bringing flowers to her every Saturday of our life together hardly made up for this selfish behavior.

Navigating Carole's family was another complicated task. After Carole left her husband and his transgressions, including alcoholism, affairs, and personal abuse, he tried to turn the event in his favor, telling their daughters: "Your mother just left you for a weirdo." When Carole and I met, her older daughter had recently finished high school and the younger was in her final semester. Both girls stayed in Oregon and lived with their father until their own marriages. While their relationship with their mother was cool initially after she left them, it improved steadily over time.

During my marriage to Carole, I reconnected with another member of my own family. You will recall from earlier chapters my older brother, Detlef. Detlef was gay, but he twice married women, each time trying to hide his true nature. One of these marriages brought his daughter, Karin, into the world. I had never met Karin — I learned years later of Detlef's divorce and that his wife had remarried an American soldier.

While I was working in the steel industry, I made a sales call on a company in Dayton, Ohio. Carole had accompanied me on this particular trip. We were waiting in the reception room, and, as I introduced myself to the receptionist, I noticed a young blond woman crossing the room. The moment was such a shock that I do not remember it perfectly, but Carole would later say that I immediately turned white and asked the receptionist if the woman happened to be of German origin. The receptionist confirmed that she was.

I spoke to the woman, and — in a coincidence that can only be described as miraculous — it turned out that she was Karin, my brother's daughter whom I had never met. I had recognized her solely by her facial similarity to Detlef. We had a nice meeting and maintained a pleasant relationship for many years to come. Sadly, my brother died due to complications of AIDS in his 50s.

My career in the steel industry had served our family well, but eventually the time came to move on. In the early 2000s, the government implemented new tariffs on steel, which made my job as a steel importer virtually useless. Carole and I decided that this was a good time for me to retire, and we left our home in Illinois for Vancouver, Washington. Our new home was just across the Columbia River from Portland, Oregon, where Carole's family lived. It was a wonderful place to be.

Our proximity to Carole's daughters, Heidi and Lisa, helped all of us forge a warmer relationship. Both girls met me and came to recognize that I was not the weirdo their father described. They could tell that I loved their mother and took good care of her. We would socialize at our respective homes, mainly at major holidays. Heidi and Lisa had their own families by this point, and we all got along splendidly.

I continued to work part-time after our move. I first became the driver of a shuttle van that provided transportation to and from the Portland airport. After about a year, I changed jobs and accepted a similar position to drive a shuttle van for the Hampton Inn hotel. A few years later, I started working for a credit card company, and a few years after that, I transferred to a different one, for whom I still work today.

From the earliest years of my life, the importance of providing for my family had been deeply engrained in me. For many decades, America offered me the opportunity to do exactly that. Ruth and Carole's partnership gave me the chance, and I will forever be grateful for their roles in my life.

Carole and I were married for 36 years. In the fall of 2015, she had a stroke and was hospitalized for a few days. Afterward, she developed serious back pain and required weekly visits to the doctor's office. By that point, she had difficulty walking, and I used a walker with a seat to transport her within our home as well as to the doctor and other trips.

In March of the following year, Carole's regular doctor referred her to an urologist, who determined that she needed an operation on three broken vertebrae. Unbeknownst to us, the doctor also took a biopsy during the operation. He called us several days later to reveal that Carole had multiple myeloma, a form of blood cancer that attacks the bones. She was referred to a local oncologist to begin chemotherapy and radiation treatment. It quickly became apparent that she needed to improve her strength to endure the oncology treatment, and she moved to a nursing home while she received outpatient treatment. Unfortunately, she did not respond well to their treatment, and the oncologist recommended that she receive more intense strengthening treatment by pain expert doctors before she continue with the cancer treatment. But even this would not happen easily. Each doctor in and around Vancouver had a waiting list of at least eight weeks, and so my extensive attempts to locate a specialist with this ability were unsuccessful.

It was always my policy to safeguard my wife's integrity by not outing myself to my hometown public. At the time of Carole's death in July of 2016, no one living in our cul-de-sac in Vancouver ever knew that Eve existed. I had made a commitment to a woman, and I had to honor it.

Chapter 7

Activism and Concealment

Until 2017, I maintained a strange but important dichotomy with regards to my transgender status. I was not "out" by any sense of the word; while Carole and my daughters had some sense of who Eve was, even my closest friends and neighbors had no knowledge of my female identity. I always believed in the importance of upholding my marriage vows, and I could not imagine doing anything that would hurt the people I care for most deeply.

Still, from the 1960s onward, my Eve persona lived an active life. I became a leader and pioneer, educating many about the meaning of transgenderism and was an articulate public spokesperson for the transgender community. I was a teacher and a supporter, providing information and understanding to thousands, both inside and outside the United States. I made over 400 appearances in college classes and at universities, approximately 20 television appearances in Boston, New York, Philadelphia, Minneapolis, Cleveland, and a few other places, and countless appearances at professional seminars and for groups of law enforcement officials and the military.

I will never forget my first meeting at the Chicago chapter of the Foundation for Personal Expression (FPE), an early organization for cross-dressers that later became known as Tri-Ess. I co-founded the group in 1965, a few years after "coming out" to Ruth. At that initial meeting, six or seven men sat together in a room at a local Holiday Inn, each of them scared to be the first one to go into the adjoining room to dress in women's clothing.

Transgender activism in these times took many different forms. On one hand, we hoped to create accepting spaces for trans individuals. As Ruth's reaction to my female attire showed, there were few places that transgender people could feel like themselves. At the same time, education was a huge component of activism. Slowly we wanted to create a world where transgender people felt like they could be themselves anywhere — or, at a minimum, would not face outright hostility.

One of the spaces where transgender people could express their true nature was at the Fantasia Fair, an annual transgender conference that was founded in 1975 and still takes place to this day in Provincetown on Cape Cod, Massachusetts. There, I helped to coordinate fashion shows and various theatrical productions. At the annual Fantasia Fair convention, I was elected Miss Congeniality, Miss Best Dressed, and Miss Fantasia Fair in 1985. At least once, Carole was kind enough to join me at one of the Fantasia Fair Conventions. With her modeling experience, she was very helpful in staging the annual fashion show. Together, we also made a two-girl team singing stage tunes. One of our favorite songs was "United We Stand," by the 1970s British pop group Brotherhood of Man. The audience loved it. Thanks to my European roots, I also became active in international outreach. I was one of three American ambassadors to the first Euro Fantasia-like convention in Denmark. We helped them with the fashion show and lectures on comportment, and shared information about everything from fashion to electrolysis.

I found Provincetown, which has been historically regarded as a safe space for the gay and transgender communities, to be incredibly welcoming. It was the first place where I felt that I could simply walk around unbothered as Eve. I am honored that my framed picture is still hanging in the photo gallery in the restaurant across the Crown & Anchor, one of the town's most prominent establishments.

I also became involved with the International Foundation of Gender Education (IFGE), a national organization that worked to improve education about transgenderism and reduce intolerance toward trans people. I became the group's national chairperson for gender education, communicating regularly with the organization's chapters to provide them with information on transgenderism and the tools to help educate others, especially the news media. The IFGE honored me with the Trinity Award in 1992, based on my lifetime service.

In 1997, the IFGE honored me with the coveted Virginia Prince Lifetime Achievement Award, named after the legendary founder of Transvestia magazine, the author of the men in dresses article that had inspired me so many years earlier. I was chosen by several thousand friends at a convention on the Queen Mary in Long Beach, California. It was moment I will never forget.

Another major highlight was the extravagant "Night of a Thousand Gowns" ball at the Waldorf Astoria Hotel in New York. The event, which still takes place every year, is one of the most prominent events for gay and transgender people in the country. I had the pleasure of attending twice, alongside several hundred gorgeous people.

Events like that one always required me to find the finest attire for Eve. To do so, I developed remarkable relationships with sales ladies at upscale department stores, such as Saks and Neiman Marcus, who were happy to help me find the perfect outfit for the occasion. I likewise made friends with the owners of several beauty shops who helped me find the perfect wigs, thereby ensuring that Eve always had a beautiful head of hair.

In addition to these conventions and beauty shows, a second major component of my transgender outreach involved presenting at colleges and universities across the United States. Prior to the 1990s, the subject of transgenderism remained largely unknown and wasn't discussed. One space that was interested in trans issues, however, was academia. Through my involvement in organizations like the IFGE and connections formed between academics, I received many speaking invitations at colleges and universities across the country. These presentations were some of my favorite. The students in attendance were always an eager audience. Many of them were meeting a transgender person for the first time in their life.

I usually made these college visits alongside my good friend Naomi. Naomi, a corpulent Jewish attorney with a sense of humor that could rival any comedian, went by Nate in her daily life. She was an especially witty speaker and would typically go first in our presentations.

Naomi's opening line was always, "Don't worry, it's not catching — it's not a disease." She introduced herself by relating that she first tried woman's clothes at age 10, when she was a curious little boy. Of course, as she grew up, she quickly realized that this was not normal behavior and hid the secret for decades. Naomi claimed that she had traditional relations with women while living as a man.

For Naomi, everything changed at a drag convention in Cape Cod when she was 40 years old and still living as Nate. A friend asked Nate to come to the drag convention to take photos. He discovered that the drag performers were decent, respectable people. After photographing the ball, he decided to try it and found it quite enjoyable. Naomi always identified more as a cross-dresser than transgender; while she enjoyed play the feminine role, she always saw herself as a man in dress rather than truly a woman.

Naomi's presentation usually lasted about half an hour, and then I was introduced. I would relate my life experience, starting with my first desire to being a woman at age 7, my life during World War II and our family's attempted flight from the invading Russian troops into Germany, and the difficult years after that as I grew up in post-war Europe. I told them about the blouse and skirt that I had carried while we escaped and explained how my priorities and life circumstances had limited my gender expression for most of my adult life. Still, I tried to leave my audience on an optimistic note, reminding them that with love and acceptance, any problem can be overcome.

Our presentations were usually followed by a question and answer session. We always made it our principle to answer any question honestly. Students frequently asked how we managed living with our alternate personas. Naomi always said that she had two different personalities: "Naomi is more outgoing, Nate is more serious." I explained how the war, my career, and my marriage vows kept me from truly living as Eve. Of all the many talks on the subject, I felt that college students were our best audience. They were always polite and interested in what we had to say. It was always a great pleasure to speak with them.

Naomi and I both lived in Chicago and were best of friends for many years. I got along well with her parents, and they always invited me to Seders, bar mitzvahs, and other family events. In these situations, of course, I was always Eberhard and she was Nate. Unfortunately, Naomi died in the late 1980s after a battle with kidney cancer. It was only after her death that her family discovered her cross-dressing tendencies, at which point I became a persona non grata for them. They did not even want me to express condolences.

In addition to talking with students, Naomi and I gave similar presentations to professional groups: medical staff, including doctors, interns, and nurses; and law enforcement groups, including about 120 FBI agents. Even the most educated people knew very little about transgender issues at the time. Educating doctors, for example, was a key goal for trans activists, as it helped to improve medical care for transgender patients.

We also did on-camera appearances at various television stations across the country, often with studio audiences. The sets were always nice and cozy, and the host or hostess would typically ask us a few questions before allowing the audience to get involved. The audiences were always very kind and interested what we had to say.

Perhaps the most wonderful part of my outreach was the people I met along the way. They included some of the most successful individuals in the country — corporate presidents, doctors, attorneys, and one of the richest women in America, all of whom had transgender tendencies that I could relate to on some level.

In the early days of my exploration of the world of transgenderism, it was difficult to meet like-minded people. Very few people were "out," and those who were, worried about what might happen if the wrong people heard about their habits. When meetings did take place, they happened in utmost secrecy. Trust was limited, and consequently so was conversation. However, I gradually developed some wonderful friendships. My transgender and cross-dressing friends and I attended many conventions together, and we always looked forward to such events with great anticipation.

At a very clandestine coffee shop in an American industrial city, I once met up with a top executive of a major firm, whom I called Susan. Susan and I quickly became friends. We shared several car trips and split lodging at transgender conventions throughout the country. In our time together, we shared our inner thoughts and deepest secrets.

When I first met Susan, she was very conflicted as to whether or not she wanted to have sex reassignment surgery. The process of reassignment surgery is long and rigorous, both physically and emotionally. First, patients partake in interviews, testing, and evaluation by a psychiatrist, psychologist, and surgeons, in order to screen out anyone who is unstable or not fit to make such a big decision. Next, patients begin endocrine and other metabolic and chromosomal studies as well as hormone therapy, if they have not already started that. Patients are often further required to live one year in their future gender role, as a way to demonstrate their commitment. After that, the surgery itself includes plastic, gynecologic, and urologic surgeries to transform the external sex organs, and follow-up evaluation and treatment that lasts the remainder of a patient's life. In summary, it is an intensely personal decision that depends very much on where one sees one's life trending.

In Susan's case, she followed my suggestion to move to Provincetown after retirement from the big corporation she had worked for. The town on Cape Cod maintained a very accepting philosophy of life even in the 1960s, and

Susan realized that she would be able to live a peaceful life should she decide to undergo surgery. This is exactly what happened. Susan had her sex reassignment and continues to live a good life in Provincetown.

Susan was far from the only friend who enriched my transgender life. Another dear friend was Karen, another friend from Chicago. Before she began to live as a woman, Karen had been Ken, a fighter pilot who flew jets for the U.S. Air Force in Vietnam. After his discharge, Ken became a pilot for Eastern Airlines, flying mainly 727 aircraft. After a few years, he took a leave of absence and had sex reassignment surgery.

After several weeks of recuperation, Karen returned to the airline and requested reinstatement from Eastern Airlines. However, the airline had no desire to reinstate her. Karen filed a lawsuit, demanding her job back. She lost the initial suit, but appealed and won the right to reinstatement. In the meantime, Karen had begun to work at the Aurora Airport outside of Chicago, handling charter cargo flights and rehabilitating a DC-3 aircraft. Then tragedy struck.

I recall the warm summer day with some great sorrow. As I was driving my car outbound on the Kennedy Expressway, I heard a news report that a DC-3 had crashed with three people on board near Aurora. Unfortunately, my worst fears turned out to be correct. The owner of the plane was about to sell it and had asked that Karen come along on a test flight. Although she was not the one piloting the plane when it crashed, she sadly died that day before she was able to return to her job as a pilot.

Another wonderful and lasting friendship was with a delightful beauty from Oklahoma named Cathy. She lived with her family, a wife and two adorable children, in a town south of Oklahoma City. She was fabulously wealthy, having inherited many millions of dollars from her father, who owned a large manufacturing company.

I am not certain about the degree of Cathy's gender identity. I would call her a cross-dresser rather than transgender. She enjoyed dressing as a woman, but I'm not sure if she wanted to truly live as one. She maintained a wonderful wardrobe and gave the visual impression of a typical, glamorous Oklahoma woman who just happened to be 6-foot-3. She owned an elaborate Prevost motor coach worth about half a million dollars, just like the ones owned by famous actors and actresses. On her long road trips, she would tow a color-coordinated Mercedes SUV. On two occasions, Carole and I had the privilege of traveling with her in style from Barrington, Illinois to Provincetown, Cape Cod. Cathy would drive up to meet us and park right in front of our house. We would load our wardrobes into the bins below the coach and make the journey together to Provincetown. Cathy made it a habit to drive all dolled up with a beautiful blonde wig completing the driver's outfit. I still smile when I recall the reaction of the 18-wheel drivers who passed her coach when they saw the white-haired woman driving the motor coach and smoking a cigar.

As they say in the southwest, the audiences "got a hoot" when Cathy appeared during the theatrical productions in her cowgirl outfit singing the classic tune "Jose Cuervo" in her hilarious, most original Oklahoma voice.

In order to discretely handle her cross-dressing adventures, Cathy secretly maintained a mobile home, which she parked in a trailer park, paying rent for the space. Cathy was also a prominent Republican in the state of Oklahoma and decided to run for the office of state senator. In the midst of a very active and heated campaign, she accidentally forgot to pay the rent due to the trailer park. The managing party decided to break into the trailer, and to their surprise, they found all of Cathy's female clothing, shoes, photos, and correspondence. The word got out and Cathy's opponents took every opportunity to use the situation as campaign leverage. Poor Cathy became local and national news. She did not win the coveted Senate seat, but her marriage survived to a happy state.

Another beautiful friendship that has survived to this day is with Dr. Sheila Kirk. Sheila, a gynecologic surgeon who practiced obstetrics lived in a beautiful home in a large mid-western city. We worked together as members of the Board of Directors of the IFGE. She was regarded as an international authority about gender and was on the board of the Harry Benjamin International Gender Dysphoria Association, which is known today as the World Professional Association for Transgender Health. Sheila wrote several books on transgender issues and maintained close relations with the medical profession on the subject. She was a prominent public speaker at many transgender conventions. She has been one of my closest friends for many decades. We frequently roomed together when we attended transgender events, and I served as the best man at her wedding. She was one of the delegates who accompanied me to Denmark when I attended the European Fantasia Fair convention there.

As I became involved with the transgender community from talks in college classrooms to conventions in Europe, I also worked to subtly change my own appearance. The fantasy of being a woman requires passing — generally speaking, this means looking like a woman to the greatest possible extent. Many transgender people will do anything possible to change their outward appearance. One of the most important aspects is the male beard, which even with make-up, is hard to cover. It simply ruins the image. In my case, while I did not have a particular dark beard growth, I invested about 2,000 hours of electrolysis for hair removal. It takes a lot of willpower to endure the insertion of a needle into each hair follicle on one's face and the corresponding electrical current that will eventually destroy the hair. I had my entire face done, as well as my hands and chest. Some treatments were even done during visits to Paris, France. The results were just what I wanted. I have not had to shave in over 45 years and my smooth skin has greatly enhanced my feminine appearance.

Many in the transgender community also use hormones to change their appearance. Dr. Sheila Kirk, my dear friend, is a notable researcher in the field of feminizing hormones; she has written several articles and books on the subject. Although hormones are not as extreme as sex reassignment surgery, they still require a thorough medical process and regular examinations. To omit any of these checkups risks one's health and may hinder the effectiveness of the feminizing process.

I began taking Premarin hormones, which contain estrogen and spironolactone, which blocks testosterone, about 50 years ago. I carefully followed a doctor's prescription. Nowadays, I have developed a 42B size breast, which eliminates the need for an artificial aid to simulate the desired shape. (Many cross-dressers or people who do not have access to hormones use bird seed for the same purpose.)

While my use of hormones brought about he changes to my physical appearance I deeply desired, they were not without side effects. One of the principle negative effects of extensive hormone therapy is the gradual loss of libido, which makes sexual relations no longer possible. As I mentioned in the previous chapter, I wish I had not had to deprive Carole of a sexual relationship due to my hormone use.

Since hormones cause physical changes, I had to be careful, as I took them for decades while I was still living as a man. If anyone in my day-to-day life did notice my physical changes, they never said anything, and I doubt they ever guessed that my transgenderism was the cause. Despite my intense involvement with the transgender community, I could not afford for my neighbors and colleagues to know my secret.

Traffic in and out of my neighborhood was always done in secrecy. I rarely left my home in female clothing to attend conventions, lectures and other events dealing with transgenderism, nor did I allow others to come to my home when dressed as a woman. Instead, I would usually change into my female role at a hotel or other provided facility. I avoided talks or conventions that were too close to our home in Chicago; I once turned down an invitation from the Oprah Winfrey Show in Chicago in order to preserve my family's privacy.

When I left the house as Eve to attend conferences, meet-ups, or the like, I always had to sneak out, and there were a few close calls. I remember one time where I backed out of the garage dressed as Eve — thinking nobody was around — only to realize that one of my golf buddies, who was quite the loudmouth, was turning from the street into my driveway. I pulled back into the garage as fast as I could and ran into the house. When my neighbor asked about it, Carole provided an alibi for me.

Another time, I was driving near our home, again dressed as Eve, when a neighbor saw me from their car. The neighbor later asked me who the woman borrowing my car that day was.

My activism and involvement introducing transgenderism to the world was a separate part of my life until Carole's death. I saw this separation as necessary to maintain my marriage vows and uphold the integrity of my partner. Throughout my 61 total years of marriage, no neighbor, colleague, or business associate knew that Eve existed. For many of my former acquaintances, the publishing of this book will be their first exposure to Eve.

Since my first involvement in outreach on behalf of transgendered issues, a lot has changed. The great secrecy that existed until late 1980s has given way to much better understanding and laws on behalf of transgender people. Today, there is substantially more information available in the medical field, and even the general public has a far greater knowledge of transgender issues. It was under this new climate in 2016 that I would ultimately come out and begin to live as a woman.

Chapter 8

Out in Venice

No two trans people have the same experience. Rather, our lives vary wildly based on differences in class, race, education, sexuality, marital status, politics, and social privilege. Our experiences are also shaped by the people who are closest to us; for me, that has always been family.

The rhetoric of "coming out" has been part of the lexicon of gay and transgender communities for decades, but coming out is much more than simply asserting that one is transgender. Coming out is a complicated process that requires us to both explore our own identities and share our findings with others. We may come out to some people but not to others, or be out only in very specific settings — as I was for over five decades. The nature of our relationship with any particular individual determines how we choose to come out and affects what happens when we are outed by others.

Many people will not understand on their own what it means to be transgender. Our only choice is to tell them more about who we are and help them understand what we go through. For many transgender people, our closest friends are the first people to whom we come out; they can also be the hardest. Many of us are afraid that we will not be accepted by those with whom we have shared so much — that we will lose relationships that have sustained for many years.

Family is a particularly complicated area to navigate. We may transition to living as female, but our children may still see us as "Dad." Hopefully, given time, they will change the way they refer to us out of respect for our transition, but it is only natural that they may also experience a certain level of grief over the change. No matter our past relationship with them or their initial reaction, coming out can also be an opportunity to establish a new relationship with adult children.

My experiences with my two daughters were different. Maureen was accepting of my Eve persona from the start, and she remains supportive today. She now lives in Berkeley, California, and she accompanied me to Caitlyn Jenner book signing events in San Francisco and Marion County when I visited her recently.

With my younger daughter, things were more complicated. Renee was 15 years old when Ruth filed for divorce and, in retrospect, she took my absence the worst. Maureen was away at the University of Virginia and Renee was left behind with Ruth as she tried to navigate high school. Contact with me became infrequent and, as time would later show, this had very negative effects on Renee. The knowledge that my transgenderism was the cause of the divorce burdened her greatly. When we did occasionally visit one another, it became clear that the gaps in our relationship had damaged it greatly. We rarely discussed Eve's existence.

After Carole's death, Renee visited me in Vancouver to console me in my sorrow. Among other things, we discussed my options for my future. I considered staying in Vancouver, close to Carole's family; moving to Berkeley to be close to Maureen; or moving to Venice, Florida, which would put me closer to Renee.

Ultimately, I decided that moving to Florida was the best option. I was sad to leave Vancouver, where I had grown close to Carole's family. Her daughters, Heidi and Lisa, and their respective families had gotten to know me in my male role, and we had developed a very strong relationship. The girls assisted me greatly in caring for Carole during her cancer treatment and were once again incredibly helpful to me as I prepared for my move to Florida after her death.

Given Renee's discomfort with my Eve persona, she and I discussed how to navigate my expression in the context of our relationship. I explained my transgender status and my desire to develop a limited female expression following my arrival in Venice. Since I had never truly lived as a woman before, I think that neither Renee nor I really understood the dimensions that this expression would take. Renee gave her approval of my limited expression, but stipulated that she not be confronted with Eve.

When I first moved to Venice, I was still very much in my male role. I quickly bought the home that Renee had scouted for me, but it was not available for another eight weeks, and Renee was a gracious hostess to me during this time.

After two months with Renee, I moved into my new home, a small but very pleasant house in a gated community. The adopted community offered an extensive social life. I attended several block parties and happy hours at the beautiful clubhouse and began to develop new friendships. Living on my own also gave me the opportunity to begin my transition into my female role.

Most of the roughly 900 homeowners in my gated neighborhood had moved to Venice from many states up north, so everyone was used to meeting new people. After about four months of living there, during which my transgender status remained hidden, I decided to test the waters. I had discovered that those attending originated from many eastern and midwestern states and everyone appeared to enjoy socializing. I had particularly bonded with some of the ladies, both married and single. The dynamic also offered me the opportunity of new confidential relationships. I hoped to share my transgender self with my neighbors for the first time in my life. My closest friends, the few people who knew of Eve, encouraged me to be myself and live the life I had dreamed of for some 75 years.

I broke the ice by inviting10ten of them to a Sunday afternoon party, without divulging the specific reason for the gathering. The party was to start at 2 p.m. I had prepared hor d'oeuvres, some wine, and the so-called Ruedesheimer Coffee, which originates in a town of the same name in Germany. None of the guests knew of the surprise that awaited them.

That afternoon, it was Eve, my trans persona, who welcomed and surprised my guests. The group was very interested in my life history, and it appeared that everyone was very supportive when they left later that afternoon.

Empowered by this success, I decided to expand my female presence and began to live full time in my chosen gender. I was finally afforded the opportunity to live the life I had dreamed of and prepared for through the 45 years of hormone treatment, 2,000 hours of electrolysis, and numerous trainings regarding wardrobe and mannerism.

Although I respected Renee's wishes and dressed as Eberhard whenever I interacted with her, she grew suspicious of my transition as she recognized some of the physical signs, particularly my development of breasts. She eventually heard from others that I had begun to live full-time as a woman — I had not consulted or informed her myself. Upon hearing such news, she immediately objected. In an email, she informed me that she was unable to continue our relationship while I maintained my new lifestyle.

I know she feels that, in many ways, I am not the father she wanted or needed. During meetings with her therapist, Renee has indicated that she loves her dad and that she was not prepared to lose him. She stressed that he has always been her "hero" and that he remained so to this day. She credited her dad for having been responsible for instilling in her positive attitudes regarding life, business, mannerism, and motivation, and that she could not accept him in his female persona. She made it clear that she did not object that Eve has complete freedom of her gender expression; she simply does not want to be privy to it. While she wants me to enjoy my new life, she was not yet prepared to come face-to-face with me, because it seems as if I am no longer her father.

Since both of us live in Venice, a town of about 20,000 people we have generally worked out an arrangement. Renee maintains a boutique and her residence on the town's primary business street, where my presence as Eve is discouraged. Renee says that she simply wants to avoid an accidental meeting in this area and prevent any negative effect on her business. I am happy to respect her by honoring her wishes. When Renee and I do see each other, I am Eberhard, dressed in male attire, not Eve.

I've always respected Renee for many attributes. She is beautiful, business savvy, and kind; she has loved me despite our conflicts. I love her dearly and suffer under the burden of our alienation. Having joined a church, I pray that time will heal these wounds.

After several months of interruption to our relationship — during which we did not speak at all — we have agreed to this détente. Whenever we plan to meet, either at her residence, business, restaurant, or on my turf, I dispense of my makeup and put on male clothes.

As you know by now, I denied my true nature for 61 years of marriage to maintain a loving relationship. At my point of life, it is of the utmost importance to me not to lose a daughter because of my gender expression. Since Renee and I reached a peaceful agreement about my expression, our relationship has become pleasant again. While I give up a small part of complete immersion into my new life, I have come to realize that while my appearance may be different for the sake of our relationship, I am no different in the expression of my lasting love for my daughter.

Except for Maureen, none of my other daughters (Renee or my stepdaughters, Heidi and Lisa) have ever come face-to-face with Eve. Their only exposure has been photos. There has never been a day when I have not loved my daughters, both my biological and my stepdaughters. I've been proud of their beauty, intelligence, and success in their pursuit of their respective careers. I'm glad that, without being presumptuous, I have the privilege of experiencing and simulating some of the life they had. I don't assume that some of their very exclusive experiences, such as childbirth, will ever be mine. The medical profession has yet to invent a solution on that particular issue. All I promise is that at age of 84, I will do my very best to bring honor and pride to womanhood.

Living full-time as a woman has afforded me the chance to participate many ordinary yet delightful happenings. Since outing my nature, I have freely participated in activities common to women. I shop for all my needs, use the services of medical doctors when needed, and participate in the social events sponsored by my gated community and the Venice Newcomers Club. I attend parties with hundreds of people in my neighborhood and have been extremely well received as a personal guest of several of my new-found friends. I attend book-reading sessions at the local library. One of the most exiting events in my young female existence occurred in June after I came out. The women's group of Gran Paradiso, my residence, scheduled a luncheon, called Woman's Day Out at the very best restaurant in Venice. Some 80 ladies were in attendance, with me among them. It was a wonderful, new experience.

When I first came out, I encountered a wave of support. These days, it seems the negligence and hostility that transgender people once faced is no longer socially acceptable in most cases. However, I quickly found that the support that people seemed to express when they first heard my news has not always prevailed. In most cases, the individual support — which was very positive at first — has diminished and, in a couple of instances, disappeared altogether. Not that anyone was expressively negative; they just no longer connected with me. What I resent most are the promises to "have lunch or dinner next week, I'll call you." In many cases, if not most, these promises are never kept. I would much prefer to simply not have such promises in the first place. It reduces the disappointment.

In contrast, the most honest and loving expressions I have experienced have come from members of the church I joined. When I first arrived in Florida, I searched the internet, more specifically Siri, for a church that might be accepting of trans people. I found the Sun Coast Cathedral, a part of the International Metropolitan Church, which is devoted to those who identify with the LGBT community.

In a lifetime of church attendance and membership in a variety of Christian denominations, I found more love, devotion, and care extended to others at this church than I had ever experienced anywhere else. I would estimate that a large percentage of the members are gay, evenly split between men and women, and there is a small number of transgender members. I simply cannot wait to attend Sunday worship every week — it is like my battery is always being recharged.

I want to keep using my experiences and knowledge of the transgender community to help educate others. I continue to share my stories and understand with anyone interested, including colleges, universities, social services, news media, police departments, and medical groups. Since my early involvement in the early 1960s, when the topic was very secretive and poorly understood, there has been considerable growth in public under-standing, but there is still so much more that people need to learn.

I realize that I am still learning, too. I had the good fortune of meeting with Caitlyn Jenner at two books signings in California. Having read her book, I see many parallels in our joint background. Caitlyn's celebrity sta-tus, the result of her gold-medal championship at the 1976 Olympics and more recent foray into reality television, position her as someone who can promote better understanding on behalf of our community. My time to do that came more than five decades ago.

I realize that my own views are evolving too. For example, I grew up seeing marriage as a unique bond between a man and a woman. When Caitlyn was on The Ellen DeGeneres Show in 2015, she mentioned that in the past she had not favored gay marriage, but she has come around to support it in recent years.

My own position is similar. Since moving to Venice a year ago, I have met many gay individuals, particularly through my involvement in the church.

Everyone with whom I have been in contact has demonstrated love, sincerity, affection, and true belief in God and scripture. Their love for one another in a married state is every bit as strong as I have observed in a marriage between a man and a woman.

I hope that I will be able to continue to provide support to anyone seeking it. Obviously, surgery at my age is not a possibility, but I am happy to just be alive and a woman.

About the Author

Eve Burchert was born in East Prussia in 1933 under the name Eberhard and today lives in Venice, Florida. This book is the story of Eve's life and survival during World War II and the years following Germany's defeat, her immigration to America and the resulting realization of living the wonderful life this country promises.

Along life's path, since age 7, Eve has been haunted by the emotions of what today is called transgenderism, a desire she denied for more of her life. At the age of 84, she adopts a new existence, identifying fully as the woman who needed to be expressed but never could be — owing to numerous circumstances as diverse as World War II, a promising career in professional soccer, immigration to America, three years of service in the U.S. Army, a 40-year career in the steel industry and 61 years of marriage.

The book details the incredible personal and moving stories of Eve's life, from the wartime years to the privilege of becoming a citizen and living a dream in beautiful America.

Acknowledgements

My thanks to Danielle Lieneman, project manager of Atlantic Publishing, and Jessica Piper, my editor, with whom I spent many hours on the phone and exchanging email messages, who tailored 85 years of memories into a form you would want to read.

Another big thank you to Doug Berry, whose technical genius was instrumental when it came to conveying my story to the reader.

My love and appreciation to my beautiful daughters, Maureen and Renee, and to my stepdaughters, Heidi and Lisa.

Finally, my unending love to Carole, my partner for 36 years, for making these years the happiest of my long life.

Works Cited

Benjamin, Harry. *The Transsexual Phenomenon.* New York: The Julian Press, Inc., 1966.

Clodfelter, Micheal. *Warfare and Armed Conflicts: A Statistical Encyclopedia of Casualty and Other Figures, 1492-2015, 4th Edition.* Jefferson, N.C.: McFarland & Company, Inc., 2017.

Prince, C. V. "166 Men in Dresses." *Sexology*, March 1962, 520-525.

Rothblatt, Martine. *The Apartheid of Sex.* New York: Random House, Inc., 1995.

Weber, Mark. "The Strange Life of Ilya Ehrenburg." *The Journal of Historical Review* 8 no. 4 (Winter 1988-89), 507-509.

Westervelt, Eric. "Silence Broken On Red Army Rapes In Germany." 17 July 2009. *National Public Radio.*